Routledge Revivals

Trouble in Guyana

First published in 1966, *Trouble in Guyana* has shown the political development of the colony against the background of clashes between personalities and ideas. For many years it was the Marxist Premier Dr Cheddi Jagan and his American born wife who led the movement for independence in Guyana. Their ambition, it was suggested, was to make British Guiana the first Communist state in South America and the Caribbean. The author knew the Jagans and other political leaders.

British Guyana became independent on 26th May 1966. Demonstrations, strikes, and riots accompanied, or led, every political development and, in the unsettled state of affairs, the British Government was unwilling to relinquish its control. However, in 1964, the ever-increasing violence became close to civil war, and it seemed possible that the Guyanese people might be irrevocably split. This book looks beyond the immediate causes, to the deep-rooted feelings of the six peoples, many of whose ancestors were brought over as slaves or, what was almost the same, as indentured labourers. It also probes the connections between Guyanese problems and the worldwide struggle between the communist nations and the West. This is an important historical reference work for scholars and researchers of colonial history, Latin American history and Caribbean history.

Trouble in Guyana

An Account of the People, Personalities and Politics...

Peter Simms

First published in 1966
by George Allen & Unwin Ltd.

This edition first published in 2024 by Routledge
4 Park Square, Milton Park, Abingdon, Oxon, OX14 4RN

and by Routledge
605 Third Avenue, New York, NY 10017

Routledge is an imprint of the Taylor & Francis Group, an informa business

© George Allen & Unwin Ltd, 1966

All rights reserved. No part of this book may be reprinted or reproduced or utilised in any form or by any electronic, mechanical, or other means, now known or hereafter invented, including photocopying and recording, or in any information storage or retrieval system, without permission in writing from the publishers.

Publisher's Note
The publisher has gone to great lengths to ensure the quality of this reprint but points out that some imperfections in the original copies may be apparent.

Disclaimer
The publisher has made every effort to trace copyright holders and welcomes correspondence from those they have been unable to contact.

A Library of Congress record exists under LCCN: 66070017

ISBN: 978-1-032-94658-0 (hbk)
ISBN: 978-1-003-58109-3 (ebk)
ISBN: 978-1-032-94659-7 (pbk)

Book DOI 10.4324/9781003581093

Trouble in Guyana

AN ACCOUNT OF PEOPLE, PERSONALITIES
AND POLITICS
AS THEY WERE IN BRITISH GUIANA

PETER SIMMS

ILLUSTRATED

London
GEORGE ALLEN & UNWIN LTD
RUSKIN HOUSE MUSEUM STREET

FIRST PUBLISHED IN 1966

This book is copyright under the Berne Convention. Apart from any fair dealing for the purposes of private study, research, criticism or review, as permitted under the Copyright Act, 1956, no portion may be reproduced by any process without written permission. Inquiries should be made to the publishers

© George Allen & Unwin Ltd, 1966

PRINTED IN GREAT BRITAIN
in 11 *point Baskerville type*
BY EAST MIDLAND PRINTING CO LTD
BURY ST. EDMUNDS SUFFOLK

TO J. F.
with appreciation

'Who did not sleep to dream, but dreamed to change the world.'
>Martin Carter: *Poems of Resistance*

'His grandchildren, perhaps, Raja grumbled, might live in a different self, or his grandchildren's children. They would have little reckoning of the womb and the curse from which they had sprung to life, and of the vast relative canvas in which they found themselves, pinpointed and cocksure like stars, as though destiny had made the past and the future theirs by right.'
>Wilson Harris: *The Far Journey of Oudin*

Preface

My wife and I went to Guyana to join a university that was about to be founded. When we arrived we found that the university was still very much of a dream and it was nearly a year before it started. The intervening time, however, was not uneventful and as a journalist I was forced to take a slightly more than academic interest in the events and personalities involved. It was in this way that the book came to be written.

Dr and Mrs Jagan helped me with material and introductions so that I could study the development of their party. Unfortunately political feelings were already running strongly, so that to be accepted by one party made it pretty difficult going with the others. But I would like to express my gratitude to Mr Forbes Burnham, then the leader of the opposition party, who, despite a feud he developed with one of my journalistic employers, was always courteous, helpful and informative. In fairness, I must say that for the first few weeks in Guyana, it was the same with Mr Peter d'Aguiar, the leader of the smallest party. Thereafter it was a question of those that were not for him were against him.

Many Guyanese have been kind enough to tell me of their own experiences in the different political parties. I have made considerable use of these reminiscences and have checked them as far as possible with contemporary documents and newspaper accounts. None can be responsible for the views I have expressed but I would like to acknowledge by name some of the many who did help me. It would be invidious to try to do more than place the names in alphabetical order, but each reading these pages will know how much I owe to his or her experiences and knowledge. They are: Mr & Mrs Peter Andersen, Sylvia Bayliss, Lewis Bobb, Moses Bhagwan, Carl Blackman, Sir Jock Campbell, John Carter, Martin

Trouble in Guyana

Carter, Mr & Mrs Ashton Chase, Dr & Mrs Bertram Collins, Ranji Chandisingh, Jake Crocker, Evan Drayton, W. E. Gocking, Richard Hart, Jocelyn Hubbard, Andrew Jackson, Ann Jardim, Lionel Luckhoo, (Commissioner for British Guiana, London) Jack Kelshall, Ian MacDonald, Frank Pilgrim, Ramkarran, Dr Fenton Ramsahoye, Lloyd Searwar, Ricky Singh, Adrian Thompson, Laurence Thompson, Clive Thomas, and Allan Young.

I would particularly like to thank Dr Lancelot Hogben, FRS., then Vice Chancellor of the University of Guyana, and Mrs Hogben for their constant encouragement and help when we were in Guyana.

My very special thanks must also go to Venetia Pollock who read the manuscript, made numerous suggestions and so willingly listened to, and suggested, new ways of presenting the material.

To my wife I can never express my gratitude sufficiently. She never complained when she herself, her dog or husband were tear-gassed, when for a month she slept in a hammock or had to run a household during long strikes or disturbances. More than all this were her valuable suggestions, and constructive help in the writing, which included all the typing, the making of notes from newspapers and other sources. I am not ashamed to repeat what so many have said before, that without her, this book would never have been written.

Kingston,
1963–65

Contents

PREFACE		9
AUTHOR'S NOTE		15
MAP OF GUYANA		18
1	*The Guyanese Mirror*	19
2	*An Interest in Violence*	22
3	*Man in a Vice*	27
4	*A Land built by Slaves*	33
5	*The Life of a Slave*	37
6	*The Despondency that came with Freedom*	44
7	*The Lowest Rung*	49
8	*So Little Reason*	56
9	*Cheddi Jagan's Story*	66
10	*First Steps in Politics*	74
11	*Gathering Strength*	86
12	*The End of Booker's Guiana*	96
13	*A Promise to Redeem*	105
14	*The Price that was Paid*	111
15	*Anti-Party Activities*	122
16	*The New Game*	133
17	*New Behaviour*	140
18	*Shifting Alliances*	147

Trouble in Guyana

19	*Refuge in Violence*	155
20	*A Second Chance*	164
21	*Points of Departure*	176
	BIBLIOGRAPHY	188
	INDEX	194

Illustrations

between pages 96–7

1a. Mr Forbes Burnham, Q.C., the Prime Minister.
 b. Dr Cheddi Jagan, leader of the People's Progressive Party.
 c. Mr Peter d'Aguiar, Minister of Finance.

2a. The Law Courts, Georgetown.
 b. The Public Buildings.
 c. Stabroek Market.

3a. The Riot Squad arrive with tear-gas, rifles and loudspeakers.
 b. 'Peaceful picketers' lie down in front of the Public Buildings.
 c. The demonstrators have become spectators and stand watching a tear-gas shell burn harmlessly in the street.

4a. Mrs Janet Jagan.
 b. Freedom House.
 c. Dr Jagan embracing two 'Freedom Marchers'.

Author's Note

Former British Colonies seem to have a penchant for initials. Certainly this is true of British Guiana but both the readers and myself would have rapidly tired of reading, or writing, such names as *People's Progressive Party* instead of the simple P.P.P. It is easy, however, to forget momentarily what initials mean, or the political standing of the groups they represent. Those most commonly used are:-

Normally associated with Dr & Mrs Jagan

P.P.P.	People's Progressive Party – at one time divided into 'Jaganite' & 'Burnhamite'
P.Y.O.	Progressive Youth Organization – P.P.P. Youth arm
P.A.C.	Political Affairs Committee, the Jagans' first political group
P.A.C. *Bulletin*	The political journal they issued – sometimes, as it is in Guyana, incorrectly called P.A.C.
G.I.W.U.	Guiana Industrial Workers Union
G.A.W.U.	Guiana Agricultural Workers Union
W.P.O.	Women's Progressive Organization

Other Political Parties

P.N.C.	Peoples National Congress. Mr Forbes Burnham's Party
U.F.	United Force. Mr d'Aguiar's Party
N.L.F.	National Labour Front. Mr Lionel Luckhoo's Party
U.D.P.	United Democratic Party. Mr John Carter's Party

Trade Unions

B.G.T.U.C.	British Guiana Trade Union Congress, often referred to as T.U.C.
M.P.C.A.	Manpower Citizens Association
C.S.A.	Civil Service Association
F.U.G.E.	Federation of Unions of Government Employees

Also

S.P.A.	Sugar Producers' Association
Guyana	The name that will be used when British Guiana becomes independent. I have therefore used it throught the text although it has meant that I have also had to follow the former spelling when using quotations or titles of books and pamphlets and organizations.

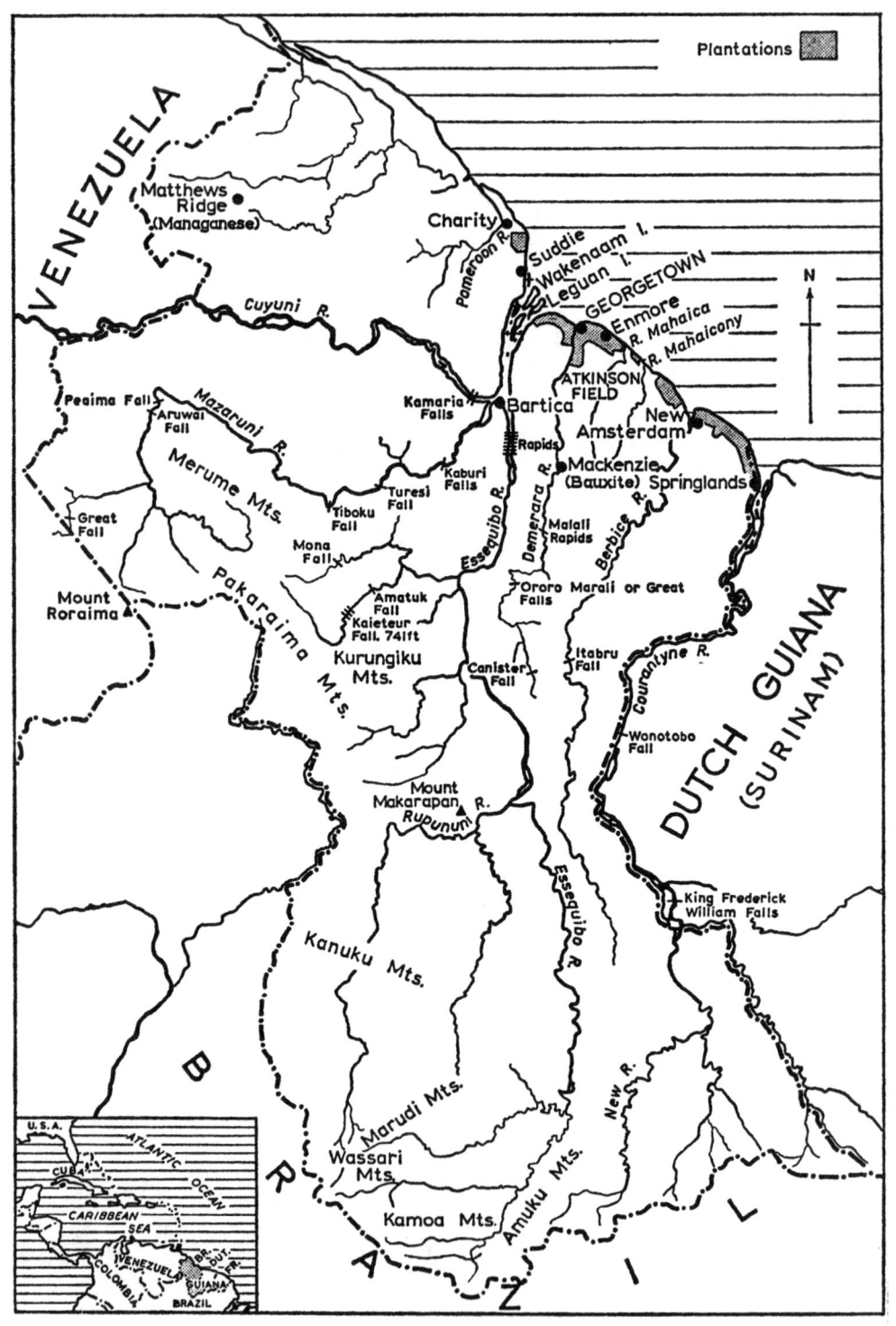

Chapter 1

THE GUYANESE MIRROR

BRITISH GUIANA is about the size of the United Kingdom with a population of only 600,000. In world affairs it must rank as a small country and, at first sight, one that is relatively insignificant. But since 1953 it has all too often been world headline news. The strikes, the riots, the bombings and the increasing inter-racial tension appeared to me, first as a journalist and later as a lecturer at the new university, as something more than the birth pangs of a nation whose gestation was taking well over a decade. For complex reasons Guyana had become a microcosm of the problems of the post-war period.

It became a laboratory where people attacked and killed each other in the name of capitalism or communism, without, for the most part, understanding what either of them meant. They sensed that there were going to be very great changes in their society, and they turned to the politicians for help as one turns to a doctor. What the politicians prescribed, and why, is the story of this book.

They were proud to boast that they were 'a nation of six races': Indians, Negroes, Portuguese, Chinese, American Indians and British. They were not interested in how, or why, their society worked. They were not, on the whole, bitter against the British who had ruled them. But changing world events had also affected the Guyanese and they looked for someone who could give form to their hopes and words to their ideas.

The man who did this was Dr Cheddi Jagan with his American born wife, Janet Jagan. Dr Jagan met his wife whilst he was studying in America. He returned to Guyana after qualifying as a dentist. While he had been away, he had changed. He had left a disgruntled boy from the sugar estates, he returned believing himself to be first a Marxist-Leninist and only second a Guyanese nationalist. He had accepted that Communism was 'inevitable' and he saw himself as the first Marxist Prime Minister in South America. This may prove to be right, but it was an act of faith that has led him into many strange byways and positions of compromise.

Dr Jagan was oblivious of the greatness of the task he had undertaken. Born and brought up in a British colony he took as axiomatic the protection that British guns gave him. He looked at the world from across the British channel. He did not ask what the United States, or his immediate neighbours might think, he did not even trouble to canvass their views.

So when in 1953 he was accused by American papers of trying to create a 'Communist beachhead' he remained sublimely indifferent, if not a little proud. When in 1962 he went to America to ask for aid he assumed that they, the people of America, would be as indifferent to his politics as if he had been the Premier of some distant land far beyond American influence.

Guyana, as the modern Guyanese now call it, is obviously tied, as every country in the world, by its geographical position. But the influences that the United States, or the Soviet Union, or Cuba, may have exerted, I have had to leave for the reader to assess as he reads the book. One Guyanese scholar has summed up Guyana's political and social isolation from its Latin American neighbours by describing it as, 'an island almost entirely surrounded by land'—an isolation that is complete, except for the occasional border dispute.

The majority of the Guyanese are, as most other people, concerned primarily with going about their business, making a living and enjoying themselves, but the Guyanese are also among the most politically minded people in the world. In general elections it is not unusual for 95% and 96% of the electorate to go to the polls. They attend political meetings with what is almost a religious fervour and they tend to idolize their leaders. Despite this, election days have always

The Guyanese Mirror

passed off without an incident and, since most of the people have long ago made up their minds, attempts at rigging or bribery have been almost non-existent. But, in between elections, the political stability of the country was constantly being thrown into turmoil and near anarchy. It was a paradox that obviously came from deep-seated causes.

The personalities of Dr. Jagan and his political opponents certainly were one of the causes. But it seemed to me that the Guyanese felt themselves to be people who had their backs against the wall. To get out of their predicament, or merely to commiserate with each other, they turned to history. It was not the history they had learnt at school, but the history that had come down from generation to generation carrying with it strong emotional overtones that set one community against another.

In the first chapters I have tried to show what people *believed* happened in their history. I have made no attempt to present a select history of the most important events. But if I have succeeded in recreating the emotional history of community memories, then the chapters dealing with the more recent events will carry with them the same overtones as the Guyanese themselves felt when experiencing them. Words that have motivated many political decisions such as *slavery, indentured labourers, plantations, Buccras* (white masters) and *ranges* (where the workers used to live), will have acquired a resonance of meaning one had not thought of before. When I first went to Guyana many of these words had no meaning to me, and, to the incredulous stares of the Guyanese, had to be explained to me. Others such as *slavery*, brought back the memory of how it was first outlawed by a *British* Parliament. This was certainly not the first reaction of any Guyanese.

To the outside world, Dr. Jagan's Marxist ideology has seemed the most important aspect of Guyanese politics. To the voters, however, it has been virtually insignificant. They have voted first for personalities and then, subsequently, for their community. I have chosen 1963, when politics were at boiling point and the people turned out into the streets, as the starting point for this account of political development.

Chapter 2

AN INTEREST IN VIOLENCE

IN 1963 British Guiana accepted organized bloodshed and violence as the only means to find a solution to its problems. To live, as an outsider, in a community that has made this decision is to know despair.

Those in responsibility continue to talk and to act in more or less the same way, becoming a little more sensitive to criticism, and a little more shrill in their own self-defence. But even while they talk, one cannot forget that some of them are actively engaged in, and nearly all are conniving at, murder.

Then there are those who are the lieutenants of the party: the man who has not spoken to you for weeks who suddenly comes into a bar and buys you a drink. You are still wondering why, when a nearby bomb goes off and you realize that you have given him an alibi. As you walk over to see what has happened, you wonder whether he is one of those thoughtful people who leave a second bomb, timed to go off just as the police arrive and the inevitable crowd has gathered.

You discover that once violence is accepted by a community nothing is the same, nobody is the same, and nothing can be relied on to remain the same for more than the instants you are actually living.

It would make it easier if you could lay the blame firmly on the leaders and their immediate followers. Certainly there is incitement, orders direct and by implication go out, but one finds that the people themselves are already infected.

There is an almost carnival spirit about the mass demonstration of the morning, but deep inside the crowd you can sense the blood-lust stirring. The crowd laughs and jokes, someone steps out in front of the police picket and calypsoes for a moment or two before slipping back into the anonymous mass. The crowd roars with laughter, even the policemen smile. But the joke is sour. Everyone knows in his heart that these are the clowns who fill up the time while the sacrificial victims are being prepared. Of course nobody as yet knows who the victims will be, nor where the sacrifice will take place, but if you are lucky you will be near when it does. If you are really lucky, it will happen right beside you.

One of the loneliest experiences is to walk down a main shopping centre in the evening while a mob is looting and the police stand drawn up at one end of the street awaiting their orders. The mob knows the police are there, that at any moment the shooting may begin, but that adds an ineluctable excitement that makes up for months, for years, of anxiety and fear. They goad each other on. They challenge each other to be the first to break into another shop. When one man, too drunk to know what he is doing, but wanting the importance of leadership, drives his bare arm through a plate glass window ripping veins and arteries to shreds, the crowd jeer at him and push him aside into the gutter while they smash their way in. They feel alive and strong, caught in an orgasm of blood and irresponsibility.

During 1963 and 1964 everyone in British Guiana became enmeshed. The fear and hatred spread out from the towns to the villages.

In the villages there was less of the mob and more of the clandestine group that worked purposefully and ruthlessly setting houses on fire with petrol bombs, arranging for people to be waylaid and attacked and sometimes beaten to death. They persuaded and intimidated others of their race to new acts of violence.

The incidents in the villages produced reprisals in the towns; so each fed voraciously on the other and the violence went on through days and months, for nearly two years.

It involved everyone, because in every household those over twenty-one had the right to vote and the results of each election could threaten the very existence, so they believed, of one group or another: the Indian sugar worker, the Indian rice farmer, the Indian businessman; the Negro Civil Servant, the Negro urban worker, the Negro unemployed; the Portuguese big business man or the Portuguese small village shopkeeper.

Everyone was involved because the differences between classes and occupations, between rural and urban societies, had been lost in the overwhelming difference between whether you were Negro or Indian.

Until 1953, the colony was treated as backward and at times, unruly. All those who had any responsibility for its affairs were agreed that the time had come for reform, and the honour for the reforms should go to the new political parties, moderate and liberal as they would be, that would come out of the first widely enfranchised electorate of 1953.

Unfortunately for those who had planned for the future, Dr. Cheddi Jagan, by then an avowed Marxist, won a landslide victory. Within 133 days the British government had suspended the Constitution and, supported by those Guyanese it had hoped would have been the elected representatives of the people, set out to create a peaceful social revolution. The old order of things patently began to give way to the new, and the majority of the people were able to enjoy a vastly higher standard of living.

But just because this revolution was partially successful, it brought a feeling of insecurity. Those who found their lives improving feared that at any moment another government might step in to take away all their newly won advantages. Those who found themselves standing still, or advancing more slowly than the rest of the community, feared they might lose even those small advantages they had possessed in the past. From 1953, insecurity was the one aspect of society that all recognized.

As well, although it was largely British money that was bringing about the revolution, the actual changes were taking place against a background of continuous agitation and incitement to strike on the part of Dr. Jagan's People's Progressive Party (P.P.P.). The Indian voter, who had for years been the underdog of the colony, asked himself whether indeed British aid and P.P.P. agitation were not irrevocably linked. Would living standards continue to rise if one had a stable government and the British government and British commercial interests no longer had Dr. Jagan's pistol at their heads?

If the Indian voter had an interest in instability, there were many others who wondered what would happen when independence came. A moderate party now, they agreed, might help the country to advance, but could there be any lasting stability until the increasing Indian population had finally dominated the Negro, or the Negro had finally dominated the Indian?

It was Dr Cheddi Jagan who led Guyanese politics from 1953 to 1964. He continued to do so whether he was in power, touring the world for international support, or in prison. His party leadership, and possibly he himself, believed that there could be no lasting power without an armed revolution. To make this possible continuing instability was necessary.

But the power Dr Jagan held did not come from Communist support. It came to him in spite of his beliefs. It came whole-heartedly from the rural Indian voter who, in thought and ambition is capitalistic, and by tradition at village level, is democratic. Jagan commanded this support because he was the only man who could contain and eventually overcome the 'Negro menace'.

In 1964 this Gordian knot of a series of left-wing governments voted into power by an ambitious right-wing electorate was cut by the introduction of proportional representation. The Indian electorate was about 48%. To allow for those Indians who did not vote for him, Dr Jagan had to pull in 10% of the rest of the electorate. This he failed to do. His party won the largest number of seats, 24, but the two opposing parties between them won 29 and formed a coalition government.

The most significant change this electoral result has brought into Guyanese politics is that for the first time the government has a vested interest in stability.

The new premier, Mr. Forbes Burnham, leads a predominantly Negro party. His government has, constitutionally, five years to run. In that time he has got to dispel for ever the fear of the Negro in the Indian mind. He has to convince the rural Indian sugar worker and rice farmer that his government has their interests at heart. He has also to keep with him the United Force (U.F.), a Portuguese and mixed party who form the other part of the coalition government.

If he cannot do these things, then even proportional representation cannot save him, since the Indian electorate is increasing faster than the others: had the 1969 electoral population voted in 1964, there is every reason to believe that Dr Jagan would still be premier.

It is easy to outline what is necessary if stability rather than instability is going to dominate Guyanese politics. But the problems in the past have proved so complex that the Guyanese have already retreated into the simplification of a racial solution. The question remains, will it be possible, despite historical, geographical, political and a host of other reasons to jolt them out of this purely racial answer—and will the different groups feel their interests are best protected and developed in a stable, as opposed to the instable, society offered by the P.P.P.?

Chapter 3

MAN IN A VICE

MOST GUYANESE will explain the causes of their difficulties by referring back to the days of the slaves or the indentured labourer. But the problem is larger than that. The very country itself is the chief opponent, defying man to make a living off its land.

Along the sea is a narrow belt of rich alluvial soil only some ten miles in depth. Behind it lies a hundred mile belt of white sands, rich in minerals but so poor in quality that, unlike the tropical jungles, it provides no form of life that will sustain man. Behind this belt are the vast rain forests and the savannahs. These too are inhospitable and treacherous.

Ever since the first European explorers arrived at the end of the 15th century, Guyana has been a land of vast, but deceptive, promises. Sir Walter Raleigh and his successors came looking for El Dorado. As they sailed down the coast from the Orinoco in Venezuela to the Amazon they were told by the native American Indians, or Amerindians as they are now called, that they had reached 'Guyana', which they took to be the name of a kingdom. Inland they hoped to find the great capital Manoa, that was said to stand beside a vast lake, its streets paved with gold and its houses decorated with precious jewels. The king was El Dorado, 'he who was covered with gold', whose riches and wealth were so great that beside them even the great Inca and Aztec empires became insignificant. The belief in this empire has been so strong that in 1924 Colonel Fawcett set off into the interior of Brazil hoping that at last it would be possible to discover its ruins and its wealth.

Trouble in Guyana

So far as one knows, there never was a Kingdom of Guyana. Guyana is an Amerindian word meaning only 'the land of many waters' an undemarcated territory divided among hundreds of semi-nomadic tribes, covered by a network of mighty rivers: the Cuyuni, the Mazaruni, Potaro, Rupununi, Essequibo, Demerara, Berbice and the Corentyne.

These rivers rise in great mountain ranges, all of which have Amerindian names, as the Pakaraima, Acarai, Kanuku and Amuhu. They flow through seventy thousand square miles of forest and untold miles of savannah.

The forests provide the bare necessity of life to the Amerindian but trees which have any commercial value are so few that only those close to the largest rivers are worth felling. They are forests of incredible beauty with bushes of Yellow Allamanda or the Red Amaryllis and the waxen petalled, night flowering, Cereus that blooms at midnight, once in seven years, and fades with the rising sun, but they are not lands of promise to hungry urban dwellers.

The great savannahs offer little immediate reward. For the most part of the year they are parched and for the rest water-logged, so that on an average each head of cattle needs 15 acres of land if it is to survive drought at one time and flood at another. Without irrigation, fertiliser and new grass seeds, they must remain rangeland that cannot be used by homestead farmers.

For the moment, the hinterland is closer to Conan Doyle's *Lost World*, a world of pterodactyls and dinosaurs that he imagined inhabiting the 22 square mile plateau on the top of Mount Roraima, than it is to the atomic and city age we know.

It might, perhaps, appear that if neither the forests nor the savannah offer any immediate hope that at least the rivers might be broad highways running into the heart of the new land. But even this has been denied. Many of these are only navigable for within thirty miles of the sea and none for more than one hundred miles. Broad and deep as they are for so much of their length, falls or rapids are such an effective barrier that they can only be used by boats small enough to be carried up the cliff faces or hauled through hundreds of

Man in a Vice

yards of turbulent boulder-strewn waters where a single mistake can mean the loss of the boat, its cargo and possibly its crew.

These, one would have thought, are difficulties enough but to the coastal dwellers it is also a land of fear. In the rivers are the carnivorous *perai* that at the taste of blood in the water go berserk, attacking man or beast. In minutes they can reduce a cow to a bare skeleton.

In the rapids and along the banks are electric eels some three or four feet long and as broad as a man's thigh. Their 500 volt shock can kill, or so paralyse a man that he dies from drowning. In the deep pools is the *camoudi*, a water boa constrictor, who lives unseen in the dark tea-coloured waters. In the shallow water of the sand banks and along the coast lie hidden the 3 feet wide sting-ray, flat and evil-looking with a two foot tail shaped like a scorpion's. Its sting is so painful and lasts for so many months, that the men who have been fishermen all their lives, having once been stung, prefer to give up their trade rather than ever risk such pain again.

On the land itself is the bushmaster, a snake that moves like lightning and whose instinct is to attack on sight; jaguar, tarantula spiders and the ubiquitous leech, all add to the fear of the interior. It is useless for those who have spent weeks or months in the forests to say that at the approach of man the jungle falls silent, apparently deserted, and, with ordinary care, one is safer there than on Main Street, Georgetown. To people brought up on the plantation, who have trouble enough with alligators and snakes in the cane fields, the dangers seem to be ever present and far removed from the life they wish to build for themselves.

So it is that these vast hinterlands support only 25,000 Amerindians, approximately four percent of the population. As well, there are a few Portuguese, and other ranchers, pork-knockers and Chinese traders. Together they do not make up even another one percent.

The pork-knocker, usually a Negro, is the romantic figure of Guyanese imagination. Too poor to get a start in life, too proud and independent to be a mere wage earner, too feckless to be employed by anyone for long and too careless to consider the dangers he is running, the pork-knocker works alone or in small groups searching for alluvial diamonds or gold. He is always dreaming, dreaming that one day he will strike it rich and find one of the pipes from which these riches stem, of what he will do with his money, of girls, of food, or unimagined wealth. In the meantime, he braves *camoudi* and electric eel and the *perai*. He risks being buried alive as he follows where the dark waters have cut deeply under the banks, searching the gravel in the semi-darkness for diamonds.

But even while he braves nature, he knows that should they strike it rich, his own colleagues may turn against him, cutting off his air supply or setting free the rope to the surface, so that there will be one less to take a cut when eventually they get back to civilization.

The pork-knocker is a haunting figure in Guyanese legend and imagination, but in real life he is a rather brash, tough, wide boy who has as little concern for your life as for his own.

There remains only two areas. The hundred mile wide belt of white sands and the ten mile deep coastal plain of alluvial soil. It is in the white sands that the country's exploitable mineral wealth lies. Guyana is the world's fourth largest producer of bauxite but it is a highly capitalized industry that has no opening for the small-time miner or entrepreneur. The bauxite is covered by 200 feet of sand and clay, ancient shorelines between glacier periods. To extract it profitably requires giant machines over a hundred feet high with vast buckets that scoop up several tons of overlay with each bite.

There are also enormous deposits of manganese and iron ore in the north-west but these too demand heavy investment and only a limited employment that is available to the technician or the skilled worker.

As far as one can see, Guyana may well be an El Dorado of mineral wealth, but minerals will never provide a direct solution to the heavy unemployment that exists today.

To live in Guyana today is to forget the rivers and the forests, the broad savannahs and the beauty of the mountains. Ninety-six percent of the population have never seen them. They live off and around a mere 480 square miles along the coast that produce two export crops: sugar and rice. These

Man in a Vice

few square miles feed them, clothe them, make some of them rich, and, hardly surprisingly, leave most of them underemployed.

Georgetown, the capital, lies some twelve feet below sea-level, so that only the roofs of the houses and the tree-tops can be seen above the sea-wall. It is a reminder that every square mile of the rich alluvial soil that now supports the country had to be won by hand. One hundred million tons of soil had to be dug by pick and shovel and moved by baskets to make ditches or build seawalls and dams. It needed a very large slave labour force to undertake such a herculean task and it is because of this that the Colony was slow to develop.

So long as life means living along the 150 miles of coastal road, scrabbling over legacies of the past, it is perhaps little wonder the Guyanese have so much unused energy to devote to politics and internecine strife.

If ever there was a country that needed to create for itself new frontiers and find new frontiersmen, it is Guyana. But this unfortunately is no new idea. Rodway in his *History of British Guiana* wrote at the end of the last century: 'Centred along the rivers and creeks lie a thousand abandoned plantations most of them indistinguishable from the surrounding forests: these represent the failures of the early settlers. At first sight the narrow line of sugar estates seems but a very poor showing for such a long struggle with nature, but when all the circumstances are taken into consideration, it is almost a wonder that the Colony has not been abandoned altogether'.

European, Negro and Indian have all at some time or the other tried to break out of the vice-like grip of the 150 miles of densely populated coastal strip where villages merge into each other and no stranger can tell the difference between where one village ends and the next begins. But all they have to show are their few square miles of arable land and the outline of 300 miles of largely unpaved roads and 90 miles of worn-out and decrepit railway.

The problem is there for everyone to see: how is the rapidly increasing population to be absorbed and how feasible is it to break out into the hinterland? There is, however, no clear cut answer.

Trouble in Guyana

To break-out requires large capital support and until this can be found to provide communications, irrigation and to clear the land, the majority of the people will remain trapped on the coastlands. To create new communities, new farmland and new industries away from the coast requires considerable capital investment in communications, irrigation and in clearing the land. It requires the type of capital that is beyond not merely individuals but also large groups. It is the government that will have to provide, at the very least, the infrastructure and the means to live through the first difficult years.

This is work that should have been started a decade ago. Until it is done, the people must remain trapped in the vice-like hold of the coasts. A movement into the hinterland does, however, offer the chance of building up multi-racial communities where energies will go to the nation as a whole, and will not be given merely to the group that, by an accident of birth, they now feel it is in their interests to support at any price.

Chapter 4

A LAND BUILT BY SLAVES

FROM the Atlantic, the approach to Guyana has none of the loveliness of the turquoise sea beating against the white sandy beaches, or the coral reefs, of the Caribbean islands. Even before the first tree tops appear on the horizon the water has turned muddy and dark, stained by the Amazon and the Orinoco, and ships still have to beat their way in between shifting sand bars and changing tides.

The silted river mouths and thick mangrove swamps must have represented an unattractive picture to the first explorers. There is no record of when the first Europeans landed nor of the first settlements. Between 1498 and 1500, Columbus, on his third voyage, sailed along the coast, but it is unlikely that he put in.

In 1620 the Pilgrim Fathers discussed the possibility of settling in Guyana and, probably fortunately for them, finally decided on the North American continent. A year later the Dutch government granted a charter to a colony that had already formed a settlement on the banks of the Essequibo, near present day Bartica. At the junction of the three rivers they built a fort, *Kykoveral*, 'Overlooking-all', the remains of which stand today.

It is probable that the first Dutch settlements grew little more than subsistence crops and were in effect trading posts bartering European goods against whatever the Amerindians brought to them from the interior. One assumes this, as their settlements were sufficiently far up the rivers to be in the infertile white sands belt. In the early period the Dutch tried to enslave the Amerindians but the Amerindian preferred to die, or be killed in captivity, rather than to work. The Dutch soon learnt that they made bad servants and dangerous enemies.

After many false starts, a relationship was built up between Amerindians and Europeans that was to last for over two hundred years. The Amerindian traded with the settlers, acted as guides and, later, after the coming of the slaves, caught and returned any that had run away. They performed this service so well that in British Guiana there is no bush Negro community as in Surinam, in spite of the number of mass rebellions with the frequent attempts to escape and to set up free communities in the forests. Those Negroes that did escape started villages deep in the forests and took elaborate care to conceal their approaches and guarded them with numerous traps. But to the Amerindian trained to the forest who can tell from a track, often invisible to a European eye, not merely how long ago and how many passed, but frequently who the people were, the Negro attempts at concealment were childish and their traps conspicuous.

Single slaves the Amerindians would bring in alone, but for the encampments the Europeans joined in the manhunt with dogs and guns. The Negro ringleaders when caught were usually killed, the planters devising the most hideous deaths, as roasting them alive or hanging them up by meat hooks, while for the others flogging and mutilation was the usual punishment.

Early in the eighteenth century the British settlers found the soil on a number of the Caribbean islands was deteriorating and, when in 1746, the Dutch declared the lands around the mouth of the Demerara open for settlement many of the British planters moved to Guyana bringing their slaves with them.

With the arrival of the British and their slaves, the two nations, Dutch and British, could bring to bear the techniques of reclamation that had first been devised in Holland and then, under Dutch instruction, had been modified and improved in the English Fenland.

The reclamation of the coastal plain is the beginning of the modern period of Guyana's history. The number of British

A Land built by Slaves

settlers soon began to outstrip the Dutch and by 1786 the colony was effectively under British control but only came under British rule after the Napoleonic wars.

The rich bar of alluvial soil that lay at, or below, sea-level varies in depth from two to ten miles, broken in places by ridges of sand. To ensure that everyone had an equal share in the costs of development and future maintenance, the Dutch parcelled out the land into rectangles and parallelograms running inland from the coast. Each planter was initially offered a frontage on the sea of about 400 yards and a depth of 3,000 yards, giving him an area of about 250 acres.

The first thing he had to do was to extend his immediate neighbour's seawall. Protected from the sea, he could then start to build dams, clearing away the mangrove trees as he went. When he reached the furthest boundary inland he had to build a back-dam. The coastal plains have two wet seasons a year and an average rainfall of 100 inches. With his plantation boxed in, he then had to start on irrigation and drainage ditches with sluices to control the inflow and outflow of the waters.

The planter had the Atlantic to his front and the floodwaters behind him. His whole life became a battle against water that could at any moment, and only too often did in the early years, break in and destroy a life-time's work.

It has already been mentioned that 100 million tons of earth had to be moved to create the plantations along the coast. But this is so large a figure that it is almost incomprehensible. A more realistic understanding of the enormous human labour involved can be seen when, as the Venn Commission subsequently worked out, it is realised that each square mile of arable land needs on an average some 49 miles of drainage canals and 16 miles of high level irrigation canals if it is to be worked.

After the planter had brought under cultivation his first 250 acres he was allowed to extend his plantation further back inland until he reached either the *pegasse*, a peaty swampy soil that quickly loses its fertility, or the white sands. The planters did not try to bring either of these soils under cultivation, but the plantations had acquired the present long narrow shape, some of them stretching seven or ten miles inland.

As we have seen, the work on the plantation began on the coast with the construction of a seawall. It was therefore only natural that the life of the plantation also grew up near the sea. The great house of the planter was built there, near him the factory and the slave quarters and the grazing land for the cattle. As well the planter had the responsibility of putting through his land the Public Road, as it is still known, that connected the estates with Georgetown, or Stabroek as it was named under the Dutch.

The whole life of the plantation lay therefore at one end and this was to entail great hardship on the workers. As the plantations extended inland, the distance between the labourers' work and their quarters also increased. In the nineteenth century the hours of work of a field labourer were set at seven hours per day. However no account was taken of the possibly seven or eight or nine miles he had to walk to work, and of the same distance that he had to cover on his return home at night. It was not exceptional, even as late as the beginning of the 1950's, for the working members of the family to be away from their quarters for fourteen and sixteen hours a day.

The slaves had built the country, and ironically enough, it was later to be an extremely difficult country for a free man to live in.

Chapter 5

THE LIFE OF A SLAVE

I TENDED to underestimate the Negro in Guyana until I had come to realize the hard facts of slavery: I began to understand that every Negro knows that sometime in the past his forefathers were enslaved. They were forced to come to Guyana against their will and under the most terrible and inhuman conditions. Once there, they lived happier or more miserable, longer or shorter lives, depending first on the ability to adapt themselves to their environment or, even more important, to chance and their master's whim. Freedom and justice may be every man's right, but they remember even today that it is not given to all. Many of their forefathers were born into slavery and died as slaves.

This is not to suggest that most Negroes spend their lives pondering, or even acting, on the thoughts of slavery, but unless one is prepared to take this past into account, to accept it at any time as an unexpected factor, one will constantly be surprised at the vigour and apparently tangential response to what appear to be perfectly simple situations.

Slavery existed in the Caribbean for over 300 years. It is impossible to summarise it accurately. But one can accept some general facts with a degree of certainty.

The first is that the slave trade resulted in the break up of organized societies on the West African coast: the prices offered for slaves by the traders made slave raiding a more lucrative profession than the reasonably stable agricultural life they had led before. Tribal warfare therefore increased just because a market for slaves had been created.

The second is that many of those who came over as slaves

had held positions of importance in their society, as rulers or medicine men, and continued to exert an influence over other Negroes, at least during their lives. But the different tribes became so mixed that the necessity to speak a common language finally drove from their memories their original backgrounds. However, the slaves did maintain a tradition of acknowledged leadership and probably had a form of hierarchy that was entirely unconnected with that imposed by the planter.

The third and the last is that although the life of a slave became gradually easier as the years passed, his master lived in ever present fear of a slave rebellion. Overnight a thoughtful and relatively humane planter could turn into a harsh, if unwilling, tyrant.

All these facts have had an effect on Negro character: he was brought to Guyana unwillingly and then freed, he feels that he has the right to expect that the society in which he lives should not, to say the very least, be biased against him. Then having lived in a hierarchy unrelated to that laid down by the plantation owner, he reserves to himself the right to his own private fantasies about his position in society. And, lastly, he believes that loyalty and gratitude must be kept within his own closely defined limits. Experience in the past has shown him that a single unrelated event, a slave rebellion on an adjoining estate, could cause his master to forget in an instant all the reciprocal obligations that he had a right to expect, leaving him defenceless and worse off than before.

If it seems difficult to believe that after more than a century of freedom many Negroes still unconsciously have these feelings, it is, perhaps, because we have not understood what it meant to be a slave.

The majority of slaves worked in the fields, but it is worth remembering that there were a number of other categories and each has also had its influence on Guyana. The house slave often lived a life of comparative comfort and could be as harsh, or harsher, to the field slaves as his master. However their lives were only a variation on a single theme, and were often equally precarious. It is the life of the field slave that made the deepest impression and has had the greatest effect

The Life of a Slave

in creating the Negro outlook on life in Guyana.

It is easy enough to find accounts of the horrors that many slaves underwent. But it is pointless to recount yet another catalogue of human crimes. Instead it seems more valuable to try to get a view for a moment of what life was like on one of the Guyana plantations at the beginning of the nineteenth century where slaves were treated without undue severity by one who must be considered a humane and Christian planter.

In 1817 John Smith and his wife were sent out to Guyana by the London Missionary Society. Their instructions were clear. They should do nothing whatsoever to antagonize the plantocracy, but should do all that they could to alleviate by Christian teaching the lot of the slave. This was in line with the Society's policy to confine its agitation to Great Britain where it had the support of both those with more liberal views, and those whose interests in the continuance of slavery were in a minority. The Society felt that local agitation might well bring retribution on the very people it was trying to help, as well as giving the planters cause to complain that the Society's work was jeopardising their lives and raising rebellion in the Colonies.

The following description is based on a long letter that Smith wrote back to the Society. It might be argued that in writing this letter Smith was providing ammunition for those at home to use. Undoubtedly he was, but there seems to be no reason to believe that he in any way twisted or exaggerated the facts to suit his, or the Society's, ideas.

Not only do other writers portray far worse conditions, but most of Smith's material appeared to be based on the life as led on the plantation at which he and his wife lived. *Le Resouvenir*, lay just to the east of Georgetown and the owner had, at his own expense, built a chapel for the slaves, the missionary's house and had also paid other of Smith's expenses.

This was exceptional and it is arguable that any owner who did this must have felt his slaves were human beings who needed not only spiritual, but also physical, assistance. The majority of the planters believed that Christianity and slavery were incompatible and, since they saw no way of doing without their slaves, were determined that the slaves must do without Christianity. The Governor of the Colony on his first meeting with Smith told him, 'If ever you teach a Negro to read, and I hear of it, I will banish you from this colony immediately'.

It was soon after writing the letter back to London that a slave rebellion broke out. Smith appears to have done what he could to avert it, but he was arrested, tried and condemned to death. He appealed against the judgement but was kept in prison under such appalling conditions that he died before the ruling that he was not guilty reached the Colony from England.

Briefly this was how the Negro lived according to Smith.

The slave quarters were usually made of frail materials thatched with leaves and enclosed with wattle, plastered with mud and sometimes whitewashed. But on some plantations the roofs were shingled and the sides enclosed with boards, which, Smith says 'have not a bad appearance'. But they were all very low, so that they were liable to flooding and must have been constantly damp and mosquito-ridden. They had no chimneys or fireplaces and windows were uncommon, such light as came in was from the doors.

The only furniture each family was allowed was one iron pot and a blanket for each person to sleep on at night. They had no tables or beds or stools and to make these, or boxes to hold their small personal possessions, they had to steal wood from the proprietor 'for which they get a flogging'.

Their food is described as 'extremely unwholesome'. The planters had early arrived at an agreement with the British settlers on the North American continent to purchase their supplies of salted cod and this on arrival usually proved to be putrid. The major part of their diet was plantain or banana. On all the estates they were, however, allowed to grow their own ground provisions. But one of the many punishments for minor offences was for the owner to set his pigs onto the slave plots and so destroy them. This was a double punishment. It meant not merely that for a while the slave was largely dependent on the food provided by the

The Life of a Slave

plantation but it took away his only possibility of earning some money by the sale of provisions to the free slaves or coloured who used to visit the plantations each Sunday.

The visit of these hucksters bringing with them cheap ornaments and gay clothes were about the only consolation the slave could find in his life: clothes remain today to the Negro one of the most important ways of maintaining his dignity as a man. For six days of the week they were slaves, but on Sunday they became men and women and could live as individuals taking pride in their person.

The planters gave them little or no clothes to work in. This was of little importance during the long hot days, but among some planters it was the practice to keep them standing in line for one or two hours shivering in the chilly night air while counts and recounts were made to ensure that they had all returned. These counts were frequently made as long drawn out as possible to give them less time to work on their own plots, so that their dependence on the plantation might be greater.

It was not surprising that illness was common. To walk around the slave quarters one would have imagined that they lived to a great age, at least if one judged by the 'mass of infirmity and decrepitude'. In fact, most slaves were old and past working at fifty and only about three in every thousand ever lived to be seventy.

The plantation hospital, like the Poor House in Britain, was designedly so bad that only the really sick would wish to enter it. It was felt that a slave who was not strong enough to get over his illness, however bad the hospital might be, was anyway not worth the keeping, and his death would mean one mouth less to feed.

Smith wrote, 'Every plantation has a hospital for the reception of the sick; though, in general, a charnel house would be a more appropriate name. It is difficult to persuade oneself they could ever be intended for the afflicted. Ventilation and cleanliness seem never to have been thought of. The excessive heat and the noxious effluvia almost produce suffocation to a person entering. There are no beds in them, the sick lie on a blanket spread on a sloping kind of platform elevated about two feet above the floor.'

Of the many punishments employed, the most common was flogging. There is no way of estimating how greatly it varied between one plantation and another as so much depended on the individual temperaments of the manager, his white overseers and his coloured or Negro 'drivers'. These last were responsible for 'driving' the men and were the foremen of the labour gangs. The whip was used frequently at work, but this was merely to encourage the lazy, or work off a bit of spite on the part of the driver, but flogging as a punishment was a very different affair.

As punishment, it was a public business and all the slaves on the estate were assembled to watch and learn. The man, or woman, was made to lie face down, spreadeagled and the wrists and ankles were firmly tied to four pickets driven into the ground. Most able-bodied men could live through a hundred lashes, but two hundred usually proved fatal, and three hundred was a certain death sentence.

A vivid glimpse of the life on the plantation, and this was in the Christian *Le Resouvenir*, can be gathered from a note in one of Smith's diaries. He and his wife awoke one morning to hear the ominous sounds of the pickets being driven into the ground. One can realise the frequency of this event, since neither at the time made any comment. Smith reproduces their entire conversation:

'When the flogging was over, Mrs. Smith said, "Did you count those lashes?"
"Yes."
"How many did you reckon?"
I said, "141," then I asked if she had counted them.
She said, "Yes, I counted 140." '

Smith records no other comment between them.

Slaves represented an important part of the capital investment in any estate and one may wonder why they were not

The Life of a Slave

looked after better. One reason undoubtedly was the constant fear that unless discipline was harsh and constantly maintained, the slaves, who vastly outnumbered the owners, would rise against them.

Another reason was the slaves were not the cowed and frightened workers many have believed. Many had an indomitable pride that they hid behind an assumed simplicity. They not only gave the least possible work, but they also did not hesitate to sabotage whatever they could. The owners on the whole believed that only by constant severity could they get from the slave a minimum of work.

As years went by fewer and fewer plantations were run by the owners. Guyana was one of the unhealthiest places in the world: yellow fever, malaria, dysentery, agues and bloody fluxes all took their due. Disease could prove fatal in hours. One young man who had newly come out to the Colony went riding and then on his return lay down in his sweat-stained clothes in a hammock on his verandah. He slept for two hours and when he awoke he was shivering. His ignorance had cost him his life and he was buried the next day. Another, a Dutchman whose estate lay in Berbice county, watched his children die one after the other. Finally his wife died also and he was left alone. On her tombstone he inscribed only her name and the terrible words: 'God Damn Berbice.'

With the increase in absentee landlordism, those who came out knew that they gambled with their lives. If they were fortunate they could make enough to retire within three or four years. On such an estate the lives of the slaves were of far less importance than the amount of work the manager could get out of them. It was in fact, as he saw it, his life or theirs and he was in no doubt over the choice. The absentee principal and the next manager could worry about replacing the labour that had been lost.

The climate, the system, the high risk and fear, all encouraged brutality. There neither is, nor ever has been, a case for slavery and although it was abolished over 130 years ago, its mark has not yet been obliterated. It will probably be many more years before everyone in Guyana can look back on it in the same way.

Chapter 6

THE DESPONDENCY THAT CAME WITH FREEDOM

IF in that three hundred year period there were many British who owned slaves, or made their fortunes from them, one must not forget the many who dedicated their lives and their careers to ending a practice that they viewed with an abhorrence and with a fearlessness that would be an example to many leaders of this century.

The horrors of slavery had been bad enough, but to the Guyanese Negro the experience of freedom was traumatic. Freedom at one time had been all he asked for, but when it came society and nature seemed to conspire together to keep him involved in a continuous struggle for survival.

In 1807, Britain declared the practice of slave *trading*, but not slave *owning*, to be illegal. She employed her navy to prevent not only her own ships, but the ships of other nations, from engaging in this trade.

This was to have little effect in Guyana. The soil was so rich that it continued to attract planters. Although slave trading was illegal, there was nothing to prevent a planter moving with his slaves from one West Indian colony to another. Owners in areas of declining cultivation tended to move from where slaves were plentiful to areas where they were in great demand. This was the loophole by which Guyana continued to receive the fresh supplies of slaves that she needed. An owner having brought them to the country was free to place them on the market, collect his profits and retire.

Finally on August 1, 1833, slavery was abolished through-

The Despondency that came with Freedom

out the British Empire. Those who drafted the Act thought it would be just to both owner and slave. It would not come into operation for one year. But from August 1, 1834, there would be an eight year apprenticeship period during which the slaves were bound to remain on the plantations but would be paid.

It was hoped that this would give the planters a chance to come to terms with their labour force and that the slaves would begin to learn the responsibilities of freedom.

It did not work out as the Abolitionists had hoped. Most planters believed that the slaves would leave the plantations as soon as they received their freedom. Instead, therefore, of trying to win their support they considered them as a wasting asset and drove them as hard as possible. They resorted to every measure they could to make the slaves so dependent on them that they could not leave. They destroyed their ground plots, they fined them on every possible occasion both to recover the wages and, more important, to prevent them from acquiring sufficient capital to set up on their own when they became free.

It is easy to criticise the planters, but many of them paid dearly for their illegal folly. One of them, a manager, in writing to his principal in 1833 has given a picture of this world that had so suddenly collapsed around him. Mr. Faloon must have been a hard taskmaster and a God-fearing man for he had a Biblical text to support his every action. He begins his letter by complaining about the 'ingratitude' of the slaves and, even worse, the lack of understanding on the part of the government magistrates.

However he and others like him had obviously spent long evenings in trying to find a way out of the calamity that had befallen them. They had, he said, 'some small comfort' in the hope that the planters would also be appointed to act as magistrates and they would then be able to inform the paid magistrate, if he were 'ignorant', of the inherent disposition of the Negro to lying and exaggeration. And in all seriousness he goes on to say they would then be able to help in other points essential 'to the due administration of justice' between Master and Apprentice. Mr Faloon and his friends did have their way, and planters were appointed magistrates and continued to sit and assist in the trial of cases in which they themselves or their friends were involved. This was to continue until well into the second half of the century.

By 1838 it was realized that the conception of apprenticeship was unworkable and all slaves on British territories were declared free. Their former owners received £20 million compensation.

How wrong those planters had been who believed that with freedom the slaves would immediately leave the plantations is shown by two facts. For one, the breakaway from the plantations lasted over 14 years, for another, those planters who had encouraged their 'apprentices' to grow cash crops and had given them land on which to build houses, managed to hold their labour force together. Had the majority of planters done this a new stable society might have grown up. But they had chosen, and even after the abolition of slavery continued to follow, a course designed to make the Negro dependent on them. As a result dissatisfaction mounted and soon a mass movement away from the plantation to the towns and the undeveloped parts of the coast took place.

A number of plantations found themselves ruined by the results of their policy, while others went into voluntary liquidation believing it would no longer be economic to work them with paid labour. During this fourteen year period twenty-five plantations ranging in size from 500 to 83 acres were sold to ex-slaves. The largest group, 168 persons, bought their plantation for $80,000 and in one instance a single ex-slave paid over $5,800 for *L'Enterprise,* a plantation of 500 acres—a surprisingly large sum for an ex-slave to possess and one that must presumably have been saved up for many years, if not generations, by a number of members of the family.

When one averages out the number of registered owners and the size of the estates bought, one finds that it gives only 4 to 5 acres for each family: enough to provide a bare subsistence level if all went well, although today it is thought that even 20 acre lots cannot sustain a family properly.

The plantations the Negroes took over became known as 'free villages'. They have been described in detail in *The*

The Despondency that came with Freedom

Approaches to Local Self Government in British Guiana by Allan Young from which the above facts were taken. Mr Young points out that the difficulties of administering the former plantations were virtually insuperable, especially for people who had had little experience of self-discipline and whose greatest hope for their future was unrestricted freedom.

Their first difficulty was to divide the land fairly. This was an almost impossible task with all the amenities, the roads, houses, and fresh water lying at one end. Then once installed on the former plantation the group had to continue to work the sluices and clear the canals for the common good. The laborious task of opening and shutting the sluice gates to meet the tides had to be followed; should it be by specified people paid by the community, or by all voluntarily? Each village tried its own solution, but none worked smoothly.

On top of this there was a considerable amount of communal labour that had to be undertaken in maintaining the canals and repairing sluice gates. Finally, and it was here that the free villages came up against the government and eventually lost government sympathy, was the need to maintain the Public Road and the bridges that had until then been the responsibility of the plantation owner. Endless discussions began, and never ended, on why the roads or bridges had not been maintained, and from whom, and by what means, the government could recover the money that it had spent in carrying out the work that the villages would not do, or had skimped.

Had there been virgin land to break in that did not need heavy capitalization, or the high degree of group administration that the intensely drained and irrigated plantations required, it is possible that the Negro would have remained on the land. As it was, the former life he had led on the plantations and the experiences of life in the free villages convinced most of them that their best hope lay in the independence to be gained by being a wage earner in the cities as a civil servant or a teacher.

The Negro started off as village constable, primary school teacher, or as an assistant to one of the missionaries. He became a watchman in government service, or one of the lower

Trouble in Guyana

grade of government clerks. He did anything that gave him a wage and an opportunity to use the little education he had received from the missionaries. In this way the Negro came to fill, at first, the lower echelons of government service that was being enlarged as, with an increasing society of free men and indentured labourers, the government had to take on an increasing responsibility in the running of the colony.

As well many of them had been trained while slaves in different trades and became carpenters, bricklayers and masons. With the coming of modern technology the Negro found his place as a skilled technician—the operator of machines and as a mechanic.

It was only later at the end of the last century and the beginning of this, that they became lawyers, doctors and clergymen.

The vast majority of them gave up any idea of either owning land or of going into business. Instead they looked for posts that although they did not give them high salaries offered them security and prestige in the community.

In this way the Negro found his place in society. And after the many difficulties and disappointments he had suffered, it was not surprising he came to believe that he had a right to it.

Unfortunately for him, more or less at the same time as he achieved this, his position was already being challenged by the very people he had despised; the former indentured labourers who had taken his place in the plantations. They, in increasing numbers, having served their indentures, were now struggling to find their own place in society.

The workers who replaced the slaves came to Guyana, at least mentally as free men. They came with clear ideas of what they wanted to do once they had served their 5 years. They wanted to make money and return to India, or to make money, buy land and settle in Guyana. Gradually the Negro came to believe that the 'coolie' whose arrival had prevented him from holding his former masters to ransom was now threatening his hard won position in society.

From these experiences has sprung, at least in part, the popular feeling that Guyana's problems are racial rather than economic or political.

Chapter 7

THE LOWEST RUNG

THE Negro was free for a few heady years, it seemed possible that he would be able to order his life as he wished, he would be able to sell, or withhold, his labour; to live on a plantation, or in a free village. As a free man he would have some leverage on society.

But the majority of the planters had early concluded that there would initially be a movement away from the plantations and only later when, because of his indolence and incompetence he was starving, would the Negro come back to the plantations.

They laid their plans accordingly, and within a year of the abolition of slavery they had begun to import contractual labour, even though it seemed then that the apprenticeship period would run its full eight years. But the planters wanted to be certain of two things: that they would be able to meet any immediate shortage of labour following emancipation, and that they would subsequently be able to break any possible monopoly in the labour supply that the Negro might try to create.

In the first years there was much experimentation. The planter playing with the idea of replacing the formerly cheap but large labour force by one that was smaller and of a higher quality. In 1835, they brought over some English ploughmen, complete with their horses, and some German farmers on a four year contract. As well, from impoverished Madeira, they indentured 429 Portuguese, and 157 other people of unspecified race from the West Indian islands.

In 1838, the same year emancipation was finally granted,

they persuaded the Indian government that it would be to their mutual benefit, if some of the unemployed in India were brought to Guyana. The Indian Government were reluctant, but, as a trial, 396 Indians were offered indentures. No more were sent until 1845 but from that year, until 1917, Indians were the main source of cheap labour for the very hungry plantations.

Throughout the nineteenth century other racial groups were imported, of which the largest were the Portuguese and the Chinese. But none proved so satisfactory as the Indian who was accustomed to a tropical climate and had a certain immunity to the two often fatal diseases, yellow fever and malaria.

Contrary to expectations the Negro did not return in any numbers to the plantations and instead a new labour force under the indenture system had to be built up. The indenturing system was open to abuse, and was abused, from the very beginning.

When he signed his indenture the labourer undertook to serve five years on any plantation he was allotted to. In return he was guaranteed a six day week of seven hours a day, if a field worker (this did not include the time it took him to get to his work and back), and ten hour day if a factory worker. Men were paid one shilling, and women and children eightpence for each day they were employed.

At the end of five years, and any additional time he had to serve to compensate his owner for time spent in jail or otherwise unemployed, he was given a certificate of exemption from labour and from that time he was free to travel anywhere in the colony and either to set up on his own, or to choose an employer.

If he had spent ten years in the Colony, he and his family, if they had completed their indentures, could ask to be repatriated free of cost. After 1885, the regulations were changed so that he had first to pay a quarter and subsequently a half of the passage money.

In broad terms these were the conditions that the indentured labourer signed on for. They were obviously hard, but they did not appear to be unjust. They cannot, however,

The lowest Rung

have given the immigrant any kind of idea of the type of life he would have to lead.

From the very moment he stepped on board ship, he entered a new society where for five years he would be under rigorous discipline and for five years afterwards, unless he had achieved the impossible and saved up a return fare, he would be lucky if he could find a wife and have any family life.

There were many hardships he would have to suffer, but perhaps the worst was that he was entering an unbalanced society. In the first years of Indian immigration only 20 to 30 women accompanied every hundred men. From 1869, the number remains above 40 but, only once, in 1900, until the last boatload of indentured persons sailed in 1917 did it reach 50—or one woman to every two men. On the plantations themselves the number of women never exceeded 71 to every 100 men.

It meant that right from the start there was trouble over women. It is hard to say whether a man was more to be envied with, or without, a wife. For one thing there was always a shortage of labour during the busy seasons and the planters used every form of pressure to make the husbands send out their wives in the *creole* gangs—gangs made up of women, old people and children who were given light work. If she were young and attractive she was fair game for the white overseer or the Indian 'driver', and until very recently, every husband knew that *le droit de seigneur* continued so long as his wife was sufficiently personable.

The law prescribed heavy penalties for anyone who persuaded another man's wife to change establishments, but heavy penalties, though indicative of the situation, did little to alleviate matters. It is indeed a remarkable, and a dreadful criticism, that such problems in Guyana's history were allowed to repeat themselves year after year.

As late as 1948, when the Venn Commission inquired into the reasons for the Enmore Riots, they found men drivers were still put in charge of women's gangs. Possibly by 1948, there was less rape by the overseers and drivers, but any woman today who is over thirty and once worked in the canefields will remember, especially when she goes to vote, the indignities she then had to suffer.

The canefields are criss-crossed by canals and ditches, and bridges were few. It is the usual practice for the worker to wade or swim across them on their way to work. For the men in loin cloths this is no hardship. But for the women under a man driver it was another problem. They still wore the sari-type Indian costume and at each ditch they were faced with either stripping in front of the man, or of swimming fully clothed, so that their clothes clung to them afterwards and remained damp or wet for the rest of the day. The drivers so one is told found this an untiring source of amusement and indecent comment.

The first indentured labourers moved into the slaves' quarters. These long, low mud-floored houses became known as 'ranges' and they remained the usual accommodation until after 1953 when the first P.P.P. government was dissolved and the Constitution suspended.

The range was a series of rooms divided one from another by thin partitions that did not reach to the ceiling. Every word, every movement could be heard so that at no time could a family have privacy . . . although possibly one is exaggerating this in importance as present day houses are still built in the same way. But what did lead to constant trouble were the communal kitchens where arguments between families were frequent and could develop into life-long feuds.

Latrines were not provided and the numerous families had to use nearby ditches that, in wet seasons, frequently overflowed and flooded the houses. Drinking water was scarce and there is little doubt that the water for washing clothes and eating utensils was frequently fouled. Such a state of affairs continued until after 1953!

This is the life that the labourer knew and when one wonders today what an Indian will consider to be just and fair one must look back and see what he then found for justice. The introduction of planters to the magistrate's bench in 1833 continued well into the century. In 1868, Des Voeux, a forthright magistrate who did much to try and bring justice to the labourer, found that even during the trying of a case that concerned themselves the planters expected to retain

The lowest Rung

their seat, 'one of these indeed was made highly indignant by my refusing to permit his whispering to me upon the subject of a case before me, in which he was the complainant.'

The labourer found that, in general the law did not protect him and that, in particular, the one man who might have shown some humanitarian feelings, the doctor, could not be relied upon.

Des Voeux in listing the different aspects that made the labourer's life so wretched says 'first as to the Medical men who attend estates. These gentlemen have the right to retain as patients in Hospital all sick immigrants, and to order for them at the Estate's expense nourishing food and medicine. . . . I fear however that there was not many who are sufficiently enlightened to take this view and I have strong reasons for believing that the food usually provided in Hospitals, in all but severe cases, is of a wretched description and this fact is well known to the medical men who dare not make complaint.

'I am moreover confident that it is the common practice of medical men to discharge immigrants before they are completely cured: and to this may be attributed a large proportion of cases of so-called idleness which is brought before the magistrates. . . . There are some well-known Managers who give out publicly that the immigrants on their Estates shall be always *during the hours of work either actually at work, or in hospital, or in goal*: a rule which can undoubtedly be enforced by the strict letter of the law, but which, invariably and rigorously carried out, inflicts extreme hardship in many individual instance, especially in the case of women who are *enceinte* or nursing young children or when the immigrants are weakened from the effects of fever and illness but being convalescent are not retained in the hospital.'

Des Voeux was writing about living conditions in the second half of the last century, but it should be remembered that although there were some minor improvements those conditions remained fundamentally unchanged until only eight or nine years ago.

It was a hard life and that there were no quick profits is

shown by the amounts that returning labourers took back with them. Although some families had saved more than one thousand dollars (£208) the average amount taken out by each person in the middle of the nineteenth century was only about $100 (£20) and by the end of the century this had fallen to under $50 (£10). As well about 10% of those embarked were declared paupers and had their passages and expenses paid. It is probable that those who chose to stay in the Colony were, if they survived, better off.

But one has yet to mention what later proved to be the turning point in Indian life. It happened in 1891. At that time there were 71,813 Indians on the plantations but, after more than fifty years in the Colony, only 33,650 had managed to break away and live off their own farms or by other occupations. Of these only some five thousand lived in either Georgetown or New Amsterdam, the only two towns of any size in the Colony: a striking example of how the Indian moved first onto the land and only when he had consolidated his position there did he move into the town.

But the importance of 1891 lay in the discovery that rice farming was a practical proposition. Rice was an ideal crop for the Indian. It could be grown in small lots, it needed no heavy capitalization, and it could be husked in small locally-owned mills. Indeed by 1905 the Colony was self-sufficient and had begun to export rice to the Caribbean. At this stage, but not until then, a large organization and capital was needed and a Rice Marketing Board was eventually set up to arrange all exports.

The Indian when he was free from his indentures had had no large estates to turn to as had the Negro on emancipation, and throughout the century laws were constantly passed to forbid the sale of Crown Lands and to make it more difficult for him to buy small plots.

Slowly the planters came to realise that the Indian did not wish to move away from the plantations where he could find drained and well-irrigated land and gradually the more restrictive laws were dropped. With the development of rice as a cash crop the Indian could at last see his way ahead. But until 1953 he was a member of a despised community, so that

The lowest Rung

neither wealth nor brains could give him a position in society and by then the Indian community was beginning to possess plenty of both.

Chapter 8

SO LITTLE REASON

For both the Indian and the Negro the past was a time of punishment and they unconsciously remind each other of this by using the word to mean anything unpleasant, or even obligatory. 'Oh, the punishment of it', they say to you in sympathy when you have just been caught in a shower without an umbrella, 'Oh the punishment of it'.

Unfortunately, however, this common memory instead of uniting them separates them even further. Even the way they refer to each other in moments of stress remind each other of the past and the socially inferior roles they then played.

In the Legislative Assembly it was not uncommon for Mr Burnham, the Leader of the Opposition, to drop into the vernacular on purpose and say, 'Me, only blackman but. . . .' and proceed to use all the skill of a trained lawyer to demolish his opponent's argument. Or again, if particularly stung by the remarks of one of the Negroes on the P.P.P. bench to interrupt by saying, 'You blackman, why you sitting with all those coolies?' Emotionally filled words, let a Portuguese or other race use them and no one would answer for the consequences.

For the Negro, the archetypal 'blackman' is someone lovable, unsophisticated, but with a native wit and cleverness that others do not realize exists. He has carefully built himself a reputation for being rather slow and dumb and of obviously giving the answer that will please his possible tormentor, but in truth he knows what is *really* happening, and is only biding his time. He is a straightforward and honest person in character, but as all the rest of the world is always taking

So Little Reason

advantage of these qualities he has been forced in self-protection to dissimulate what he feels. Since he makes no pretence about his dissimulation, it is not a vice but a temporary attitude imposed upon him.

And the 'coolie' for the Negro? Sadly enough he is not lovable. For one thing the Negro had to be forced into slavery and kept there by punishment and torture. As soon as he had an opportunity to be free he took it and left the hated plantations. But the coolie what did he do? He was a free man and he sold himself voluntarily into the same conditions that the Negro had had to be forced into. Also, by doing this, he prevented the Negro from ever holding the planters to ransom by the withdrawal of his labour. Without coolie labour, the planters would either have had to employ the Negro on his own terms, or else have gone bankrupt and left the colony in his possession. It was the 'coolie' who stole the Negro's birthright when emancipation finally came.

And again, look at the coolie! He is devious. He is not straightforward. When he begins to earn: he does not spend his money so that he can enjoy life with clothes that make a man, or in the rumshops talking like a freeman. No, for years he goes on living in apparent penury, wearing old fashioned shabby clothes, but all the time he is renting or buying pieces of land, until suddenly one finds that the poor and despised family down the street is a hundred times richer than you are and using its wealth to build up more. And now with better living conditions and a more stable society his birth rate is far ahead. Soon more than half the Guyanese people will be Indian and will run everything to suit themselves. Against people who so patently ignore all the accepted rules of the game, it is difficult to compete fairly.

And how does the 'coolie' see himself? First he comes from a country with a proud history and tradition and though there is no caste system in Guyana nearly every Indian will tell you that he comes from a Brahmin family. Life in India was hard and coming to Guyana meant that he was prepared to face even greater immediate hardships with the knowledge that, if he survived, he would have the opportunities he could not find in his own country. He knew that life would not be easy, but he was prepared to accept this. Yes he lived like a slave, but was that his fault? If there was any fault it was the fault of those who reduced him to that condition. But even while he was being treated like a slave he was mentally a free man. He was obtaining land, he was building up a little capital. He was building a new society.

Nearly everything was against him, the planter, the government, nobody wanted him to break free and when he did break free, when he became a respected member of society, a large businessman in Georgetown, or a large rice farmer, even then society shut its doors. There was a chance for a Negro to sit on the Governor's Committee for this and that, on the Red Cross, on the Library Committee but it was almost impossible for an Indian. One must look at his other qualities. For years he put back every penny he could into land, or his business, so that he had a settled position. Then while still badly housed, still cheaply clothed, he spent his money on his children, giving them the best possible education, feeding and clothing them properly. Later he was able to give them respectable houses, so that they need never be ashamed as he had been. It had been one long, uphill battle. When Cheddi Jagan came, he had stirred up society so much that out of self-protection it threw open its doors to any respectable Indian and then, later, to any Indian who belonged to the P.P.P. Also Cheddi Jagan broke open the door to the reserved posts on the sugar estates, he backed the rice farmer and rice became an integral part of the economy. In fact he made the Indian.

And what about the 'blackman' for the 'coolie'? The blackman lives for the moment. He will accept anything, if he thinks that he can dress himself up on Sundays, if he can sit and talk in the rumshops. He is lacking in social integrity, he has no family unit. When he was a slave, the planters encouraged promiscuity so as to increase the birthrate. And now the blackman has taken on two values from the *buccra*. He wants promiscuity to begin with, then later he wants to be married in church, even if, to have the kind of wedding that he thinks fit, he has to wait twenty years – and half the bridesmaids who are holding up his wife's white tulle train are their own daughters. For years the blackman has been the person who ruled their lives as policemen, post-master, drainage inspector and most important of all as the clerk that you had to deal with whenever you had to get something from the government. Well, now the blackman has got to recognize there are other values and society is changing and there will be more Indian policemen, more Indian civil servants, and Indians can deal with their own kind.

So across the trenches of history the two races face each other. And, like all armies, each is certain of the righteousness of its cause and also certain that whatever obvious advantages the other has, it has some intangible advantage of its own that will ensure it victory.

The Portuguese and the Chinese also suffered under the indenture system. The Portuguese were among the first labourers to be brought over in 1835 and continued intermittently to be offered indentures until 1882. Most of them were virtually destitute when they arrived for their standard of living had been miserable in their home country. Even so, the life on the ranges so appalled them that both they and the Chinese turned their backs firmly on the plantations as soon as their period of compulsory service was finished. They were determined, whatever the price, to make their future independently of the planters.

The Portuguese, like the Negro, were to find it difficult to make a start in the community once they had accepted freedom. But they did have the advantage of being one of the first peoples to be brought into Guyana under indentures and they had an opportunity to go in to business against little or no competition. Having won this position they were able to help other members of their family or fellow countryman that followed them over to expand and consolidate the small advantages they had gained.

The slaves had been provided with everything that was essential to maintain life. His cash crops were used to buy his only luxuries: Sunday clothes, rum, tobacco, and sweetmeats. The hucksters, usually women, who ran this trade were manumitted slaves or free coloured. They required very little capital, had no shop nor need of organizational skills. They prepared food in their own houses and then walked or rode to the plantations to sell it.

Once contractual labour had been introduced, the worker was naturally required to provide everything he needed out of his own wages. The large quantities and range of goods obviously could not be transported daily backwards and forwards by the hucksters. Village shops had never existed before, but with the ever-increasing number of paid labourers they became a vital necessity.

Possibly by lack of skill and capital, certainly by temperament, the Negro huckster was not able, or willing, to create these shops and it was this opening that the Portuguese took as soon as he was free.

In doing so he was to alienate himself from both the Negro and the Indian. From the Negro because the hucksters found themselves unable to compete with the village shop and therefore saw themselves deprived 'by the Portuguese' of a living. From the Indian because as farmers they needed long credit terms to get them over the difficult periods between sowing and harvesting. The high rates of interest and the control that the Portuguese shopkeeper could exert over the Indian's spending, as well as or the inevitable slights, real or unintentional, between the Portuguese creditor and the Indian debtor have not been forgotten. Nowadays most of the village shops had moved into Indian hands (who incidentally charge just as high a rate of interest). The Portuguese have either become owners of wholesale firms, department stores or light industries, or else have become wage earners, especially shop assistants, or entered the Civil Service. Like the Negro, the Portuguese sought refuge in the towns and as a community has suffered from the perpetual under-employment that is a so much more serious problem for the town dweller than the countryman.

Although the Portuguese were fortunate to gain an entry into business in the early days, they have always tended to feel bitter at not possessing the prestige that attached to other white men from abroad, nor the acceptance usually given to early immigrants who feel they 'belong' to the country. In this they have had the worst of both worlds.

So Little Reason

The Chinese too moved away from the plantations as soon as their indentures ended. Many in fact, relying on their tightly knit family ties and greater organizational ability frequently fled the estates before they had served their full term.

Those who decided to remain agriculturalists were equally determined to be independent. They therefore left the rich alluvial lands where they would have had to work with the planters or other races to run the complex drainage system, and, instead, moved up the creeks of the Demerara and Essiquibo rivers onto the land that the Dutch had first settled. But, like the early settlers, they found the soil was soon exhausted. Few of their villages are in existence today.

Others went further into the hinterland and opened stores for the pork-knockers, advancing them food and equipment at such extremely high prices that they virtually became partners in the enterprise, standing to make a great deal of money if the person they staked struck lucky and nothing at all, except the possibility of staking him again, if unlucky.

Some Chinese moved into the towns, always holding onto their independence by maintaining themselves at the lowest possible level and ploughing back everything into their business. Their instinctive preference for a high turnover and a small profit, and their willingness to stand by a bargain, even if it subsequently proved disadvantageous to them, won the respect, if not the liking, of the other races.

The community now numbers about 3,500 spread through the Colony. The smallness of its numbers and its chameleon-like qualities have led it to a strict political and racial neutrality: although its instincts probably incline more towards the Indian than the Negro.

Many of the older generation have never spoken, or else have forgotten, their language. But in recent years with increased wealth, it has become the practice to send their children first to Hong Kong for a year or two and from there to China. In China they have been encouraged to see themselves as Chinese and to learn the language. It is not unusual to find a son and daughter speaking to each other in Chinese as they work in their shop, while their father and mother still know only English. Whether these young have also acquired a political consciousness, along with their language, remains to be seen.

The last of the 'six races', is the British. It is for a Guyanese to write one day what the British were really like, and to say what the Guyanese people feel about them in retrospect. But the P.P.P. landslide victories of 1953 and 1957 must, and can only, be taken as popular criticism of British rule. It is only necessary to remember how the Indian labourer still lived, some thirty years after the indenture system had ended, to see where this feeling came from.

However one will not explain popular feeling by merely putting it down to 'exploitation'. The British community was divided into three groups, and each group had its own particular influence.

The first was obviously to the Governor and his government. His was ultimately the source of all prestige and he was the fount of all social honours. Although a great deal depended on the personality of the Governor himself, he was not entirely free. He was also dependent on his Colonial Service officers and the leaders of big business who were firmly entrenched in their positions of power.

Big business meant the London directors and the managers on the spot, who were expected to get results. Part of the farewell speech made by Sir Gordon Lethem on giving up his post as Governor in 1946 is quoted later and in it he gives some indication of the power they wielded. He remarks that the bauxite industry during the war seemed 'to expect almost exemption from the ordinary operation of civil government' and went so far as to forbid His Majesty's Commissioner of Labour from visiting their plant . . . and were successful in doing so.

The other, and largest, British group were those salary earners who worked for British business. In the sugar industry most of them did not have any great educational background. For them work in a Colony meant starting at the bottom and acquiring the skills that would take them up to the top, or at least to a position of responsibility, with the possibility of

So Little Reason

retiring to England with considerably more money than their parents had ever had.

If they stayed on they had to be consciously, or unconsciously, willing to accept the *status quo*. From the beginning they were made to realize that they were fortunate and there were dozens of others willing to take their place. One person remembers how he would be sent out by the manager to ride ten miles to check whether a sluice gate was open or not. It was a pointless task, other than keeping him in his place, but there was no avoiding it as the manager would take care the next day to check with the sluice gate operator whether or not the overseer had been there. You accepted discipline and you therefore expected the workers to accept discipline. It took a person of exceptional moral integrity and perspicacity to accept the difference that whereas he would one day go on to be a manager himself, the workers had hardly anything to look forward to.

One of the worse aspects of British rule was that it was a rule of privilege and that merit could only carry a Guyanese so far. After that the doors were shut, regardless of whether he was better qualified than the Englishman who was doing the work. It is difficult to see why the government helped to send students to England when they could not obtain fellowships, even though they deserved them, nor on their return, positions of responsibility. It was so obviously bound to lead to discontent.

One double first at Cambridge found on his return that the Education Officer was strongly of this exclusive outlook and refused to give him any post in a government school. For some years he was forced to run a private school until at last he was given a post at Queen's College in Georgetown . . . hardly, one feels, the best use a double first could be put to. Another obtained firsts as an agronomist but on his return he found by the evasive replies that he got to his applications that agronomist positions were reserved for the British, even though many of them had far lower qualifications than he had. Eventually his father sent him back to England with instructions to study law. Again he did brilliantly and has risen to the top of his profession . . . unfortunately however, when he first returned any gratitude Britain might have earned for herself tended to be lost in his disappointment at having to follow a career not of his own choosing.

Each of Britain's three classes affected the Guyanese: the Governor and his staff, the big business managers, and the professional and technical employees. By closing the doors to the higher technical and managerial posts, Britain forced the best brains of her colonies into two professions: law and medicine. Law offered both the greatest possibilities for social and financial gain and was therefore vastly over-crowded. In this way Britain gave to her political opponents men who by training and ability were ideally suited to speak to the people, to organize them, and so to lead them that they took advantage of everything that the law allowed . . . and, if they were arrested, to stand up in court and defend them. It was an explosive legacy.

Guyana was a small and largely forgotten country. It was run by a closed oligarchy under pressure from its masters at home who tended to take the short-term and narrow view of any situation. Even in 1953 the long, coastal strip where most of the wealth and the population lay was nothing more than a tropical Gorbals, an enormous slum from which the under-privileged – whether Indian, Negro, Chinese or Portuguese – could look across at the seemingly impregnable positions of the British and a carefully selected few Guyanese.

Only in these terms can one understand the post-war swing to the left by both the intelligentsia and the worker, and only thus can one see why even people who are now his political opponents, say that modern Guyana must be divided into two periods: the pre-Jagan and post-Jagan eras.

It was Jagan who showed that the positions were no longer impregnable who so put the fear of god into the directors of Booker's that they appointed as their Chairman a young and junior member of the Board, Mr Jock Campbell (now Sir Jock), a Socialist whom they hoped would save something out of the cataclysm.

He was to do more than that. He completely changed the outlook of the company and the conditions of the people on the estates. But once change has set in, not even the most

So Little Reason

radical innovations can catch up with people's wants, nor did Dr Jagan, riding the crest of the discontent he had aroused, ever feel that he could for more than a moment let it appear that real progress was being made. He could discuss co-operation between his government and Booker's, but he could not let it be seen that togther they were implementing a joint policy. For Dr Jagan the dichotomy of the past was the strength of the present, and he gambled on the hope that it would continue to be so in the future.

What Dr Jagan's policy finally brought was a state verging on civil war where all issues were reduced to race: the Indian against the Negro, with the other races throwing in their weight as they thought their best interests lay. Dr Jagan had forgotten that while he spoke in terms of class warfare, the people themselves were thinking of what they knew of the past and were wondering what each development meant for their future. In this the Indian and the Negro had different viewpoints.

Chapter 9

CHEDDI JAGAN'S STORY

IF Cheddi Jagan has not written the history of Guyana since the war, he has certainly jogged the elbow that held the pen so often and so insistently that he, ultimately, is responsible for the shape it has taken. The interesting questions are whether, with the power he won in 1953, he could have turned the course of events in the way he wanted?

Did he even know what he wanted? Or was it some fault in his character that then, and subsequently, made him spend much of his energy undermining his own position?

Did his inborn qualities of leadership combined with his childhood of near poverty, and his failure to win academic distinction, develop in him a feeling that though he could lead, he could not win?

He was born on March 22, 1918, at Port Mourant, the largest village on the Corentyne. Both his father and mother were indentured labourers, earning between them three shillings and fourpence for each working day. In a year their total income from the estate was probably never more than thirty pounds.

Their first years in Guyana they spent in a range like any other immigrant, but by the time that Cheddi Jagan was born, they had managed to rent a long ramshackle kind of house with a mud floor, walls made from bits of corrugated iron – beaten out flat to make them as large as possible – and a roof thatched with banana leaves. They did not have any furniture but with some rough boards they made two or three platforms standing about six inches off the ground. During the day they could sit cross-legged on these to eat, and at night time they served as beds. They had one or two brass bowls for eating and drinking out of and that made up their household possessions. For many years rice bag sacking was all Mrs Jagan could afford to use for making clothes for her children. It was also the only kind of covering they had as blankets on the beds.

The old house has now been pulled down and a new one, raised off the ground on piles, has replaced it. But Mrs Jagan still continues to rent the same piece of land from the sugar company, still looks over the same canefields, still has to walk down the same muddy lane outside the house to get water, and still lives among the millions of mosquitoes that breed among the small ditches and swampy patches in her garden. In the two wet seasons, her garden is still covered with water as it used to be.

Admittedly the family was once poor, but is it still necessary for her to live on the same swampy bit of ground, still fight the sugar company to give them something better than a standpipe from which to carry their water in buckets to the house; to fight over the fact that the lanes are still not properly drained, so that the water forms great pools that have to be crossed on rickety planks. Is it pride? It is certainly not for propaganda. Or is it a Jagan trait to keep yourself in a position where you are always making a frontal attack, always slogging at an invincible, because intangible, enemy?

Mrs Jagan certainly has no love for the sugar companies. When she describes her early life, it is a re-creation of the life one has read, in general terms, of the indenture labourer. But she carries the livid scars of those days and turns up her sleeves or pulls back her skirt to show where so many innumerable times the cutlass slipped as she worked cutting cane.

When one has spent an afternoon talking to Mrs Jagan, one has no doubt that she was the dominant personality in the family. It was she who was determined that her sons should go to the best schools, whatever the immediate sacrifices that had to be made by the family. It was she who rented land, who took out insurance policies on the older members of the family and turned the capital gains to some purpose. It was also she who encouraged Dr Jagan's father so that he became one of the drivers. These are no mean achievements when one has started with nothing but a roof, rough boards and a mud floor.

She was also determined that Cheddi Jagan, her eldest son, should not have to work in the canefields. He was a quiet person who enjoyed reading, or just sitting listening to people, or using his hands. He passed creditably through the junior schools and by 1933 he had finished at Port Mourant High School. He is reticent about those days but says that he remembers how even then other boys accepted him as a natural leader and was surprised to find how he could so easily make them follow him.

There was only one good secular college in Guyana; Queen's College. It was then reputed to be the best in the Caribbean, and any student who did well had a very good chance of getting to England. There was also the annual Guyana scholarship, which Forbes Burnham later won, that would have sent him to England and paid all his expenses there. The family decided that Cheddi should go to Queen's. To do this they had to borrow money to provide him with respectable clothes, a mattress, and each month they had to send him money for his tuition, lodging and food.

But when he had finished in 1935, the sacrifices appeared to have brought little more than an increase in prestige. As a scholar, Cheddi Jagan had been only of average standard and he says today, 'When I left Queen's College, the only things I was fit for, were to teach, or to be a clerk in the Civil Service – nothing else. And I was determined that I would rather starve than work for the government as a clerk.'

He went back to Port Mourant but he could only get odd jobs that seemed to him to lead nowhere. At one time his father thought he could get him to set up in a small business but Cheddi refused. He was on the point of surrendering to his parent's wishes when two friends told him that in the United States the fees for a course in dentistry were very small and if he could borrow US $200, he would then be able to earn enough money in the holidays to keep himself in the States for three or four years.

Cheddi Jagan's Story

By this time the Jagan family had a reputation for being responsible. His family were able to borrow the money for him and he left for Howard University, Washington, and later Northwestern University Dental School, Chicago.

For the first year, he says that he still had no particular purpose beyond his curriculum and the need to find odd jobs to keep himself alive. During one vacation he sold patent medicines in New York. In Port Mourant he had learnt how to cut trousers and in Chicago he went to work in a hock shop turning trousers that had not been redeemed to make them look better when sold. He worked as waiter, lift-boy – and all those other part-time temporary jobs one can find in a city.

Formal education had never caught his imagination. But two things happened to him in Chicago. The first was the life in the neighbourhood around him. It had been a white area and was gradually being taken over by the Negro. As he saw the changes and listened to the people as they grumbled, he could see before him that society was fluid and changing. It was not immutable as it seemed under the planter's rule. He began to feel that he should take an interest in social problems and started going to evening classes at International House, Brent House and the Y.M.C.A. One of the lecturers, an Indian, was a believer in the Gandhian methods of civil disobedience combined with non-violence. Here Dr Jagan's political thinking began. It is perhaps here that one finds the fundamental dichotomy in his early and later political studies that was to cause his political action to swing so uncertainly between two extremes: violent or peaceful revolution.

Dr Jagan has either forgotten, or else is reticent about, how his studies developed. But at some period he began to read the sensational exposés of the capitalist system as *The Rubber Barons, The Lords of the Press* and similar works that both he, and surprisingly Janet Jagan, still speak of with respect. The influences of these books was to be lasting: especially the technique of piling one quotation on top of another regardless of original context, so making the enemy condemn himself with his own words.

It was these books that fired Cheddi Jagan as nothing else in the past had. He says that it changed the world for him. He saw the enormous differences in wealth between different peoples, he saw what could be said and done in Guyana and his imagination started to work. He began to look for new outlets and found these in political meetings and discussions.

But, perhaps, he would never have been anything more than a dentist interested in political questions had he not met his wife, Janet Rosenberg, during his last year in the States. They met at a party and began discussing politics and went on talking far into the night. The handsome, extremely charming and photogenic, Guyanese student and the fine featured and beautiful blonde girl were, with their different talents, to provide an unexpected and for some time unbeatable combination.

To wield such power as was to come to her is to demand comment, and people have not been slow to produce a background for Janet Jagan. The first point of departure has been that she was related to the Rosenbergs who were executed for spying for Russia. Janet Jagan usually raises this point when she first meets someone and says that she is always grateful to a rich Indian, of one of the opposition parties, who spent thousands of dollars employing a detective agency in Chicago to find the connexion and, by his failure, proving that it did not exist.

Much paper has also been spent on stating explicitly, or merely by surmise, that Janet Jagan was, in 1943, a member of the Communist Party. She has denied this categorically throughout her public career, but on the other hand has made no attempt to disguise her liking for Communist ideals, nor during her visits to the Soviet Union and China has she disguised her admiration for their system.

It has recently been suggested by an American writer that she did not belong to the Communist Party, but to an affiliated organization, the Young Communist League. He draws the distinction that whereas a member of the Communist Party lives under the party discipline and is sometimes clandestine, a member of such affiliated organizations is not under discipline and is certainly not clandestine as his or her value rests in action, or propaganda work, that is done openly. If this is true, it would explain much of how and why first the political group, and then the party, the Jagans formed behaved as it did. Other than that the whole question must, if one has read the two political journals they subsequently edited, *P.A.C.* and *Thunder*, be academic.

Cheddi Jagan's position is less academic. His political philosophy, as outlined in speeches and private conversation, is full of innumerable contradictions and it is often he who in press statements has been responsible for the international picture of the P.P.P. as a Communist organization.

On such evidence as is available, it seems probable that when he left the States he was closer to civil disobedience and non-violence, but that he was drawn to Communism by the force both of what he had read and what he had heard in discussions with Janet Jagan. Subsequently his views hardened, but then there were other complex reasons that induced him to call himself a 'Marxist-Leninist', a label that nobody, including Dr Jagan, has been able to explain coherently. The reasons for this may perhaps come clearer as one watches his political career develop.

In 1943 Dr Jagan gained his degree in dentistry and with it the honorary title of Doctor that, in Guyana, is accorded to all professional medical men. In August he married and two months later left for Georgetown to break the news to his family and, one guesses, to raise some money for his bride's fare.

In December, Janet Jagan who had been studying nursing, 'it seemed a patriotic thing to do in those days', left the United States with one silver dollar and her ticket. Breakfast in San Juan used up most of the dollar and by the time she arrived she had nothing left.

As soon as Janet arrived they went to Port Mourant to meet the family and to be recognized as a part of it. This can have been no easy thing to do, since to the Jagan family, Cheddi had probably wasted most of their investment by coming back with an American wife (a liability) rather than immediately getting down to starting a practice and allowing them in their own good time to arrange a marriage for him with some family that was richer than they, but lacked the social position he had won as a dentist. As well, they must have expected someone who would be utterly alien, in every sense of the word, to their life.

But they had no idea of the kind of person Cheddi Jagan had married. The first thing Janet asked was to be told in detail how she would have been expected to behave had she been an Indian wife. She then told her mother-in-law that firstly she expected to be treated in exactly the same way and, secondly, she expected to be corrected and told when she had done something that was wrong.

Probably the family received the request with some scepticism, but Janet had made up her mind, and she is, when she wishes to be, a most determined woman.

In those days it was quite unheard of for a white woman to subjugate herself in this way. For this is what it entailed. She spent her days with the other women in the household, either in the kitchen, or in the bedroom, or sitting outside. The sitting room had to be left free for the men so that they could talk freely about politics or whatever else interested them: these were two worlds and they only impinged at certain times and in certain accepted forms.

As well, she did her part in the household work and did not expect to be waited on. From an Indian point of view, it was all unbelievable. This was the beginning of the legend of the 'blue-eyed Bhow-gi' . . . the 'blue-eyed sister-in-law' as she came to be called in the Indian community. Instead of losing face in Indian eyes, her prestige increased steadily. She retained the prestige of a person with a foreign education, but for the first time she, a white woman, was shown to be more than sympathetic: she was prepared to live the same life and to share the same hardships. Then it must be remembered that very early on both Cheddi and Janet had began to talk politics – the kind of politics they spoke about had never been heard in Guyana before, nor the kind of promises they made, nor the things that they told people 'they had a right to'. While Cheddi Jagan spoke to his men friends around the sitting room, Janet Jagan spoke to the women across the kitchen fire. The political lessons they expounded began to give them additional influence.

They returned to Georgetown and eventually found a room

for a surgery on Main Street, and, with some difficulty, they acquired the relatively expensive instruments that a dentist must have. Once they had settled, they turned to politics again.

Cheddi Jagan had a bicycle and with Janet Jagan riding on the cross-bar they began to visit trade union leaders, to attend meetings and participate in a series of weekly discussions that were taking place at the Public Library.

It was in this way that they began.

Chapter 10

FIRST STEPS IN POLITICS

THE personalities of Cheddi and Janet Jagan were to dominate the progressive movement in Guyana. Because of this, many accounts have tended to see them, quite incorrectly, as the sole founders and the originators of this movement and have also tended to accept that, when the party passed through a critical time, their policy decisions were necessarily correct.

One must remember, however, that throughout the 1930's the West Indies Committee of the Communist Party, from its offices in London, had, with West Indian intellectuals, been actively concerned in the affairs of the area. The foundations for a progressive movement had already been laid in the colony and even then were being extended by the contacts made with Guyanese students in London.

When the Jagans settled in Georgetown one of their early preoccupations was to learn about the trade union movement. One of the first people they went to see was Jocelyn Makepeace Hubbard. In the window of his shop was a copy of Palme Dutt's *The Problem of India.* Perhaps they did not realize it at the time, but the fact that Dutt's book, with its Marxist interpretation, was there, symbolized the foundations that had been laid in the past, that they would be able to use in the future.

Having said this, one must then accept that it was they who were prepared to mobilize what lay dormant and create whatever the future might demand. To begin with there were two things that had to be done if a progressive movement were to be formed. First they had to identify and bring together those with leftwing views and those who were

First Steps in Politics

prepared to work for leftwing causes and then, second, to find positions where they would be in contact with the workers.

Jocelyn Hubbard helped to introduce them to trade unionists and those of the left. He proved to be an indefatigable worker and a selfless and faithful supporter. As well, the war had stimulated new ideas. A group of liberal and leftwing people met regularly at the Public Library for lectures and discussions. The Jagans attended these for a while and so got to know many of the politically-minded in the city. Those they believed to be leftwing, they collected around them.

They worked hard in trade union circles. In September 1944, Jocelyn Hubbard wrote *The Workers' Study Circle Committee Members Manual*, a guide for those who would be prepared to arrange lectures for them and to help the Workers' Committees make use of the study material the Jagans would provide. But the Workers' Study Circles needed constant support and never developed any momentum of their own.

There were two major unions that the Jagans wished to gain control of. The first was the oldest, the *British Guiana Labour Union*, formed by H. N. Critchlow in 1922 and still dominated by him. Critchlow had been a water-front worker and, dissatisfied with existing conditions, had set about forming an organization to give him and his fellow workers the power to better their conditions. His union, both in its outlook and organization, was formed on the British pattern.

The second, the *Man-power Citizen's Association* (M.P.C.A.) had been started by Ayube Edun, one of the most remarkable Guyanese characters who, perhaps because of his warmth and old-fashioned ideas about the British Empire, has not yet had the credit due to him. He, like Cheddi Jagan was born in a range and he too felt a responsibility to go abroad so that he could come back and improve the lot of his own people. But he was a romantic and because he was a romantic, he could find no existing political creed that would satisfy him. His stay in England produced instead a book, in every line of which his personality shines through, and a philosophy that he thought was so rational that every country would eventually adopt it. He believed that it was England's destiny to provide the leadership the world needed.

The book, *London's Heart-Probe and Britain's Destiny*, is largely an account of what he finds on his visit to London in 1928. He begins, and this is worth quoting not merely to show his own character, but also to introduce some balance to the descriptions that have already been given of the life the plantation workers lived: 'I am a British Citizen by birth – a fact in which I glory. I was born of pure-Indian parentage, in a distant outpost of the British Empire, on a sugar plantation, far away in British Guiana, the only British possession on the South American mainland, in a home that had for its floor the bare earth'.   He goes on to say that since his task was principally concerned with the working man he felt it his duty to travel as they did – steerage. It was not a pleasant experience he notes and comments on the appalling stench of the lavatories that were partitioned off from their mess room. But in the evening he forgets this when he goes up on deck to think about man's inequality and the great division between rich and poor. He wonders what he, a poor Indian, can do to change things.

He delighted in classifying whatever he saw. When he arrived in London he was perpetually noting how things worked, 'The visitor's first impression of London is the immense traffic'. He concludes that there are three strata of streets, the first stratum is represented by New and Old Bond Street, Regent Street and Piccadilly. There the pavements are almost empty, except for some sightseers, and the traffic is largely Rolls Royces with aristocratic occupants. The second stratum is Oxford Street and New Oxford Street up to Holborn, Cheapside, Poultry and the Strand and there are more people. But the busy crowded streets are in the third stratum, Tottenham Court Road, Charing Cross, Kingsway and Edgware Road.

So he goes around, noting that English people have bad teeth; that in the public lavatories there is always a compartment marked 'Free', but 'I have observed that before using the free lavatory, the user will glance around to see if there are any acquaintances nearby, for no sooner is he known to

First Steps in Politics

have used a free lavatory than is shunned by companions as a "down and out".'

He is struck by the marvellous courtesy of the serving class. He remarks on the then two extremes in British life: the few who are rich, the many who are poor. 'British aristocratic life is full of luxury, extravagance and pleasantness. The King and the Royal Family and Courts represent the acme of culture and gentility. . . . The Royal Household derives its support from a Civil List granted by the British Parliament. No member of the Royal Family does any work'.

So he looks and records, noting that the English are 'dog mad', as they are mad about sports. He considers the problems of feeding London, and of educating the people. He is a Pepys, who notes everything, however small and insignificant.

Then in the last twenty pages he comes to his theory. 'I have endeavoured all along to bring to the notice of the reader the findings of my probing at the heart of London. . . . Great Britain has led in the vanguard of civilization. It has ceased to lead for a decade. What is the reason for this?'

He suggests that the social order in Britain has outlived its day. He turns to Russia and, after explaining how the new order has invigorated the society, he says that the price in human lives and freedom is too great to be paid. Instead society should be organized by the functions that its members perform, there should be a *Rational-Practical-Ideal* State, and, with the Guyanese love for initials, this becomes the R.P.I. State.

At the top is the Supreme Council of Intelligentsia, under them Transitory Intelligentsia, then the Man-power Citizens (Man-power of Brain and Hands), then the Women Citizens, the Children, Disabled and Retired Citizens. He expected that the society would be inaugurated by those who would one day constitute its Supreme Intelligentsia using non-co-operation, passive resistance and Civil Disobedience, but never by shedding blood, nor by any act that would be treasonable to the government in power.

If Britain started this, he believed that other countries would follow so that one day all the nations would be united and on 'One Great Memorable Day' each year everyone in the world would hold mass meetings and 'with bare heads, pay homage to an UNKNOWN INTELLIGENCE'.

His book was published in London in 1935, but the response was disappointing, the British intelligentsia did not step forward. Undaunted, but realizing that the Guyanese intelligentsia would be a little more than he could tackle single-handed, he decided to start with those whom he knew best and needed his help most. He turned to the Indian plantation workers and for them, since they were, in his ideal state, the Man-power Citizens, he founded the Man-power Citizens' Association to build their place in society for them.

He was an inquisitive, observant and sharp-eyed, if idealistic, critic. He must have met with many rebuffs, but he took them and never became sour or disgruntled.

Edun, by then, was not a plantation worker and his founding of the M.P.C.A. encouraged others with less noble ideas to build their own personal empires by starting trade unions. Many of the unions that were formed later were at the instigation of people in totally unconnected professions. There was nothing unusual therefore when Dr Cheddi Jagan, a dentist, joined the M.P.C.A. nor was it surprising that he rapidly became its Treasurer.

Dr Jagan did not wish to forward the R.P.I. State. Within a year of his gaining office, the M.P.C.A. split and the next year (1946) the Guiana Industrial Workers Union (G.I.W.U.) was formed by Dr Lachhmansingh and Amos Rangela, both ardent Jagan supporters. The G.I.W.U. sought its membership among exactly the same workers as the M.P.C.A.: the Indians on the sugar plantations.

Dr Jagan had not gone into the M.P.C.A. with the intention of splitting it. He had certainly wished to gain control of it. In 1946 Jocelyn Hubbard was elected to the critical post of Secretary to the British Guiana Trades Union Congress (B.G.T.U.C.) and Cheddi Jagan and other of his supporters all obtained union posts. Jagan's work among the unions was never to be really effective and, as a result of his failure to understand the problems involved he twice tried to push through a Labour Relations Bill, that would have given the unions he was interested in power. In 1953, the Bill helped to

First Steps in Politics

precipitate the suspension of the Constitution and in 1963 caused an 80 day general strike that brought with it the violence that was to continue well into 1964.

The reasons for Jagan's failure in the unions are probably twofold.

The Guyana unions are based on the British pattern. The demagogue can be carried a long way towards the top by his popularity by the rank and file, but once he has reached the inner circles he is among hard-headed pragmatic men with their own particular interests and views to defend. Flexibility and a willingness to compromise, in order to maintain support within the group, are essential and these qualities, so far as one can see, Dr Jagan either did not possess, or did not understand. Dr. Jagan once told me bitterly, in a private conversation, that in those early years as he tried to get a footing in the unions he found constantly that he was being stabbed in the back and that people whom he thought he could trust were bribed to leave him. Others have said that the trade unionists recognized that Dr Jagan was out to dominate them and closed their ranks.

But the second factor the Jagans did not recognize, either in those early days or later, was the workers' ambivalent attitude towards the unions. In the *History of the P.P.P.*, Janet Jagan writes. 'The M.P.C.A., trade union of the sugar workers, began with a "bang" and caused high hopes to spring up in the hearts of the long-neglected and long-exploited sugar workers. This hope was soon destined to die when its leaders took to the golden path of bribery and sold out the rights of the workers.'

There is no doubt that many workers believed this, but they could see a clear division in their interests. They were prepared to accept that the M.P.C.A. had become a company union, but it had managed to keep a steady, if small, increase in wages, or prerogatives, and it certainly prevented any violent abuse of such rights as the workers had won.

The Jagans promised them far better things if they were put into power, but these were only promises and no one could be certain that the Jagans would get power.

In union matters the workers therefore tended to give their

support to the M.P.C.A., or even to both M.P.C.A. and the G.I.W.U., so re-insuring against the future, but in politics they gave their votes to the Jagans. If the Jagans won and could pull off their promises so much the better, if they lost, then the workers would still have a bulwark in a union that knew how to deal with the big bosses.

The Jagans had by this time met, and won as a supporter, a brilliant young Negro trade unionist, Ashton Chase. He was to continue his career as a unionist and with the help of a scholarship to Ruskin College was later able to take a degree in law which he now practises. Chase understood the need for conciliation and compromise, but his influence among the unions was not enough.

On November 6, 1946 two important events took place. The first was that the Governor, Sir Gordon Lethem, gave a farewell speech to the Legislative Council. He had been there for five years and was due for retirement. But there are many who think that had he been permitted to stay on he would have marked out Cheddi Jagan, who was to win a seat in the Legislative Council the next year, as an up and coming man and would have guided and supported him. He might, they argue, have so won his trust that Jagan would have been a moderating influence in his party, and there were certainly many moderates who would have given him the fullest support. However, Lethem departed and this must remain one of the question marks of history that cannot be answered.

The second event, of more long-reaching results, was the publication of a duplicated weekly called Political Affairs Committee (P.A.C.) *Bulletin*. The *Bulletin* was the first unifying force that the Jagans created for those who were prepared to accept their political beliefs and to act with them. The founder members were the Jagans, Jocelyn Hubbard and Ashton Chase. Around these four and their *Bulletin* was to grow the major political party for more than fifteen years of Guyanese history. The *Bulletin* was to run for 43 issues and only died when P.A.C. was turned into a national party. On its masthead it listed its aims as:–

'To assist the growth and development of the Labour and

First Steps in Politics

Progressive Movements of British Guiana, to the end of establishing a strong, disciplined and enlightened Party, equipped with the theory of Scientific Socialism.

'To provide Information, and to present scientific political analyses on current affairs, both local and international:

'And

'To foster and assist discussion groups, through the circulation of Bulletins, Booklets and other printed matter.'

Scientific Socialism is, of course, the term Marx and Engels used for their political philosophy, or in other words, Communism. This was later to be dropped, and when the P.P.P. came to be formed it appeared as a national liberation party.

But P.A.C. was still a small relatively unimportant body. It seemed to be less important than a new party that had been formed by Dr J. B. Singh, O.B.E., called the British Guiana Labour Party. Raymond Smith quotes him as saying at the inaugural meeting. 'Tonight I am introducing to you a Political Amalgam of our Racial groups in British Guiana'. It was a Labour Party formed after the English pattern and would certainly have won support from the British Labour government had it not been so cleverly disintegrated by P.A.C.

Its existence did, however, highlight one deficiency of P.A.C. P.A.C. had the following of the more progressive intellectuals of Georgetown, it could probably command large support, but it could not guarantee mass support from the Negro: it was not an amalgam of the racial groups.

The signs of racialism were growing, but for the moment the Negro did not feel threatened by the Indian, who, although he could feel his mounting strength, was still the despised race. Mr Brindley Benn, a Negro and former P.P.P. Minister, says that he can remember at that time how the Negro hucksters used to bring their produce into Georgetown and be met at the ferry landing stage by waiting Indian porters who carried their goods to the market. The Negro women would show their disdain for the Indians by throwing a tip on the ground so that the Indian had to grovel for it.

Trouble in Guyana

There was, and always had been, racial antagonism, and people would be likely to vote for the party that they felt best represented their interests.

If the P.A.C. was to create a popular movement, it had to be certain that it had someone who could swing the Negro vote. I know of no documentary evidence that will support the following, but many people who were then concerned in Guyanese affairs, have told this same story quite independently, and throughout the West Indies it is accepted without any shadow of doubt.

It is said that the British Communist Party were perturbed by this weakness in P.A.C. and began to look around to see if they could help. They picked on Forbes Burnham, the Guiana Scholar of 1942, who was to prove one of the most able and pugnacious lawyers Guyana has. Burnham was then either a member of the Party, or very close to it, – in writing this, let us remember that many people were then (1947) impressed by Russia's fighting in the war and attracted by her violent anti-colonialism. They saw in Communism a force that could be used to help them win independence. Subsequently, and some of these remarks are given later, Burnham was to state that there was no intention of trying to turn the P.P.P. into a Communist party, and those who put Communism before independence were worse than fools. It may also be said that the Commission in 1954 listed Burnham as the leader of the P.P.P. moderates.

However, whatever Burnham may have thought about Communism and whatever the British Communist Party thought of him, it was put to Dr Jagan that this defect of not having a popular Negro leader had to be remedied and that Burnham was the only person who could do this. Jagan accepted and made Burnham an explicit promise that he would be Chairman of the party they were about to form, and, by implication, that he would therefore, be the leader of the party. This was later to have disastrous repercussions on the P.P.P., but it did at the time ensure Negro support for the yet unborn party.

But that was far ahead, since it would be two years before Burnham returned and in that time the form of the new party would have to be worked out. The immediate problem, which was directly linked with this, was the elections, the first since before the war. These were to be held under a limited franchise in November 1947.

P.A.C. had started off with the intention of being the nucleus of a Scientific Socialist party. But in 1947 it was still only a group of people of divergent views. A few were dedicated leftists, but for many this was the opening that was to lead to independence or to the creation of their own political career. It therefore suited everyone that the P.A.C. did not fight the election as a party but as a collection of individuals. This went so far that when the *Sunday Chronicle* on the day before polling ran a list of the candidates, it headlined the Jagans at the bottom of one of the pages as:

Jagan versus Jagan

It then commented, 'Dr Jagan and his wife Mrs Janet Jagan, stand, more or less, on similar platforms'. The 'more or less' suggests that there were noticeable differences and whereas Dr Jagan is listed as an 'Independent Labour' candidate, Janet Jagan and the other members of P.A.C. have no label at all.

Although the elections were held under a limited franchise, all the races would be voting and the results of the election would show how much of a following P.A.C. could command outside the Indian fieldworkers. Janet Jagan to try to bring in a multi-racial vote had formed during that year the Women's Political and Economic Organization (W.P. & E.O.) which she calls 'the first real political grouping of women' – although in her *History of the P.P.P.* she incorrectly post-dates its creation to some unspecified date after 1950. Most important of all, she started it with Mrs Winifred Gaskin, a Negro journalist and writer who is now Chairman of Burnham's People's National Congress, the P.N.C.

There were fourteen constituencies to be contested, for which there were thirty-one independents, including members of P.A.C., eleven members of the Labour Party, seven of the M.P.C.A. and the one Independent Labour candidate, Dr Jagan.

On the day before polling the *Chronicle* gave very considerable prominence to six of the independents, only one of whom won a seat. It gave a box to the Labour Party and one to the M.P.C.A. Other independents got their mention and then, last of all, came the Jagans. None of the platforms was very radical, except that the Jagans said they would fight for the elimination of nominated seats and the Recall System, if indeed one can consider these radical moves. The Recall System, was a favourite concept of the Jagans in those days. It gives the right to voters of any constituency to 'recall' their candidate at any time if they consider he is not voting in parliament as they wish. They can then demand a bye-election. This deters any candidate, who does not have strong personal support in his constituency, from crossing the floor, or voting against his party, since in the bye-election the party would give its support to a new candidate and he would lose his seat.

The results of the election were to be indicative of how future electorates would respond. Of the thirty-one independents only seven won their seats. The Labour Party gained six and the M.P.C.A. drew zero.

Looking at it another way:

Dr Jagan won his seat in Central Demerara because it was an Indian sugar workers district;

In the urban, and therefore non-Indian, constituencies:

Janet Jagan lost in Georgetown Central to a Portuguese businessman, 'Honest' John Fernandes;

Jocelyn Hubbard lost in Georgetown North to Dr Nicholson, a Negro with strong racial feelings;

and Dr Lachhmansingh came fourth in Georgetown South with 173 votes, the only candidate he beat was supported by the M.P.C.A. whose votes totalled 16!

The results of the election showed that P.A.C. might have the Indians and intellectuals in the city on their side, (although by no means all, as Leon Schuler, a strong left-winger and former member of the P.A.C., actually stood against Janet Jagan), but they certainly did not have the Negro, Portuguese, or coloured votes.

The M.P.C.A. lost all their seats and should have learnt then that the Guyanese do not mix national politics with their union membership, even Ayube Edun came a poor second in his constituency.

The Labour Party should have learnt that it had paid them to stand together and that the electorate was obviously turning radical. But the Party, for all its high-flown statements, was in truth only a loose formation that had formed an electoral alliance and had no programme or common ideals for the future. Even so, it presented a threat to P.A.C. and Janet Jagan set about destroying it.

To do this she used the P.A.C. *Bulletin* in a most effective series of articles. Whenever a Bill came up before the Legislative that could be presented as of major importance to the lives of her readers she described its advantages and disadvantages in the clearest and strongest terms. If the issues were sometimes over-simplified, that was not, perhaps, so important as their being clear-cut. She then listed how the different members voted. She proved that Dr Jagan consistently voted for the people, while the Labour Party she showed to be hopelessly split and, by constant repetition, to appear as frightened and sycophantic followers of the ruling class.

Under the strain the Labour Party disintegrated and by the next election the P.P.P. picked up the leftwing votes while the rest were divided among the other parties, or went to independents.

So Dr. Jagan's political career had begun and Mrs Jagan had lost her American nationality by standing for elections in a foreign country.

Chapter 11

GATHERING STRENGTH

IF Dr Jagan could not catch the tone of the trade union inner circles, he showed from the beginning an understanding of parliamentary life. He also showed considerable moral courage as he consistently put forward views that he knew would not be popular with his colleagues.

The Legislative Council was formally opened on Thursday, December 18, 1947 and on Friday 19th he asked his first question. It concerned an increase in pensions and he wanted to know how much would be going to England to retired civil servants living there. The Colonial Treasurer in his reply said, 'I may state the hon. Member was courteous (enough) to inform me beforehand and so I had the figures prepared for me'. It was the first, and one of the very few occasions, when he was thanked by one of the Nominated Members.

At the third meeting on January 6th, he made his maiden speech on the budget. He did not escape unscathed.

He began by saying that he would like to reply to the Governor's speech on the day the Council was opened, 'and I would also ask permission to read the reply of the British Guiana Labour Party.'

THE PRESIDENT: The hon. Member is reading it as a Member of the Council and not on behalf of those Members belonging to that particular Party. What is the object? The hon. Member can go on speaking as a Member of the Legislative Council.

DR JAGAN: I am speaking as a Member of the Council. I also want to state that several Members are also members of the

Gathering Strength

Party, and if we can give the other Members of this Council an idea of what our programme is, it would be valuable.

He then read out a seventeen point policy statement by a party he did not belong to, had never campaigned for, and was determined to destroy. Its members recognized him as someone who would be a constant embarrassment to them, yet somehow, within a month, he had obtained such moral ascendancy that he had made himself their spokesman. It was no mean achievement.

He said that the Labour Party was 'disappointed' that no specific mention had been made of plans for Industrial Development, and threatened that they were going to expose some rather unpleasant facts about the coconut industry. He then fired two brisk salvoes against the Colonial Treasurer.

They disapproved of the Treasurer advancing sums of money without prior approval from the Legislative Council as the Treasurer had just done to a private airways company. This should stop.

He then went on to say that they had observed that the Honourable the Colonial Treasurer had adopted the usual procedure of under-estimating the possible Revenue, 'which later gives him the opportunity of presenting a series of supplementary estimates to cover up lamentable failures on the part of those concerned to properly estimate the cost of the projects in hand. . . .' He pointed out that when the Treasurer came to Customs Revenue he admitted he could not even call his figures 'a guess'. But why then should he give a figure of $4.6 million which was so obviously below the $6.6 million of the year before?

The eleventh point he must have enjoyed making: 'We desire to point out that there is still too much leakage when new taxes are to be introduced, and it is time that Government do something to put a stop to it' . . . one in the eye for those very moral up-stage Colonial Office administrators!

He complained on the behalf of the Labour Party, as he was to complain for years, that the bauxite companies kept their profits low in the producing country to reduce taxation and by arranging prices between inter-locking companies could so arrange their accounts that the highest profits were shown in the country where they would pay the least taxation.

He got himself into a muddle over how the Dollar Pool worked, and allowed himself to be corrected by the Colonial Treasurer, even though he was most probably on the right track. But he kept going until he decided to show that big business was making large profits that were not being shared with the workers. He employed the technique he had learnt from *The Lords of the Press*, he quoted:

'For every £1,000 made by the rich in 1938. . . .'

THE PRESIDENT: What is the hon. Member reading from? What is the document?

DR JAGAN: I am merely giving a quotation from a paper.

THE PRESIDENT: What is the paper?

DR JAGAN: A paper of Statistics from the United Kingdom.

THE PRESIDENT: If the hon. Member wishes to quote anything he must state what he is quoting from.

DR JAGAN: It is just a paper called *The Communist Party Industry Special* (laughter).

THE PRESIDENT: Hon. Members should know what importance to attach to it.

DR JAGAN: Hon. Members may laugh but these are facts on figures. I shall proceed:

And so he went on, bravely, sometimes a little ineptly, sometimes a little naively, until he ended:

'With those remarks I propose to take my seat, but before I do so I would like to say that I observe that a provision is made in the Estimates for a contribution of $600 to the Society for the Prevention of Cruelty to Animals. I wish that this government would set up a Committee for the prevention of Cruelty to the working class people of British Guiana.'

Not a remark that was likely to win him friends in Government House, but if anyone at that time had thought it worth considering the speech, it was certainly one of a man who was not afraid to express his opinions in correct parliamentary form. Also it was certainly not the speech of a rabid demagogue. Again one must ask the question, without hope of an answer, whether, had Dr Jagan been encouraged to develop the parliamentary side of his life, he might well have been more moderate.

But this was not to happen. The proceedings show that in the Legislative Council, he took beating after beating, he was snubbed and laughed at, but he always came back for more.

Instead he was to have the chance of making political capital far more easily.

P.A.C. accepted as an article of faith that they had to win control over the unions, but they refused to learn from experience. On April 5, 1948 out of 30,000 sugar workers (this includes maximum seasonal labour) the M.P.C.A. had a registered membership of 6,000, while their union the G.I.W.U. had only 60. To increase membership they would have to prove themselves more militant and stronger than the M.P.C.A.

A year before in June 1947, complaints had been made to the M.P.C.A. both about the system for cutting cane and the payments made. The practice in Guyana is to set fire to a field of cane before cutting it. This clears out any snakes and small alligators and also removes the dry sharp-edged leaves.

Until 1945, the system had been for the workers to be divided into two groups. The more senior were the cane cutters. They were paid by what the overseer estimated the cane on the field weighed. This seems an impossible task, but both overseer and cutters developed a very fine expertise. Before the cutting started, the overseer would give his estimate and the cutters if they disagreed would argue it out. Obviously much depended on personal judgement, and some overseers would be frightened of giving too high an estimate for fear of offending their manager.

The other workers used to pick up the cane that had been cut and load it into the punts. They worked in groups and were allotted numbered punts.

In 1945, the Labour Commissioner, after innumerable complaints, got both management and workers to agree that the men should both cut and load. When the numbered punts arrived at the factory a worker's representative would

Trouble in Guyana

be there to check the actual weight of cane delivered. The men would then be paid for this.

It seemed fair in theory, but in practice, the men complained that it was tiring to have to change from cutting to picking up the cane and carrying it; that often there were not sufficient punts and they wasted time waiting for one to arrive; that the scales at the factory were not just; that the planks leading up to the punts were slippery and dangerous for the older men; and that the companies had introduced a new variety of cane that had a higher sucrose content but weighed less, so they were losing.

It was not until February 1948 that the M.P.C.A. decided at a conference with representatives from every estate that the men did favour 'cut and load' but they wanted to be paid $1 a ton instead of 60 cents.

The Sugar Producers' Association finally agreed to 85 cents on April 15th. On April 17th there were 6,999 people at work in the field and factory. In the last week of April the G.I.W.U. called a strike and by May 8th the labour force was down to half, by May 22nd only 2,645 were at work. The largest drop was in the Indian fieldworkers and as a result many of the factory workers were on short time or had been cut back. But a week later the strike seemed to be ending, there were 3,159 people at work, by June 12th there were 3,929. Official opinion was that the strike was broken.

It was about this time that trouble began. On June 10th, the strikers on one estate drove people at work out of the fields. On June 15th at *Non Pareil* the Head Overseer and one other overseer and nine labourers were beaten up. The next morning at *La Bonne Intention*, the Head Overseer, a Mr Mitchell, was beaten with sticks and then forced to walk barefooted and bareheaded, carrying a red flag through the estate. When he got to the front of the estate he had to be taken to hospital.

But the real trouble was building up around Enmore factory, a neighbouring estate to *Non Pareil*.

On the evening of June 15th the Manager of the factory rang up the Police Superintendent to tell him that there had been a meeting held by Dr Lachhmansingh's group and the

Gathering Strength

decisions had been made to go to the factory the next morning and beat up anyone who tried to go to work. Mr Payne, the Manager, added that the factory at the moment held large stocks of rum and he was worried in case the strikers broke in, and getting drunk, became uncontrollable.

A little while later, the Assistant Manager heard what he described as a 'zooming' of the telephone wires and Enmore and *Non Pareil* were cut off.

Georgetown was informed and during the night a police lance corporal and six constables all armed with rifles and ten rounds were sent to the factory to help the local force of one lance corporal and six constables armed with batons and another lance corporal with three armed constables.

At half-past five in the morning the police heard a whistle blown and the noise of a crowd approaching. It was led by a man named David Alfred who had first turned up at Enmore in the middle of April, just at the time when the M.P.C.A. reached its agreement with the Sugar Producers. Nobody knew where he had come from, but within a week he had told the Manager that he was one of the workers' spokesmen and he played a prominent part in the meetings held by Lachhmansingh and the Jagans.

After the rioting that took place on June 16th, he disappeared and although the Commission of Inquiry attempted to serve him with a *sub-poena*, he was never found or heard of again.

L/C James estimated the crowd at about 400 and he said they were armed with sticks, iron bars and cutlasses. They milled around the factory gates and assaulted some workers who turned up until the police advised the workers not to try to enter the factory.

The Superintendent arrived with his baton men and the crowd was persuaded to go away. As they left the police heard them say that they were going to *Non Pareil* to destroy the bridge and then would come back to enter the factory.

The Superintendent, whose territory covered some forty miles of the Public Road including seven sugar estates, appears from the subsequent evidence to have been so exhausted by the strain of the previous weeks of strike and trouble that he was no longer capable of thinking clearly. He decided to leave the three lance corporals at the factory, without, however, putting any of them in charge and taking a jeep set off with his County Sergeant Major and two armed constables to *Non Pareil*. When he got there all was quiet and he decided to go back to his Station Headquarters to report to Georgetown. He and his Sergeant Major took no further part in the troubles that were about to overtake Enmore.

Soon after the Superintendent's departure some of the canefields began to burn. This is always a sign of defiance, as once the cane is burnt, it must be cut within two or three days – after a week or ten days the sucrose content is so low that it is useless. Unless the estate can get its workers back within that short time it stands to lose thousands of pounds.

Then about ten o'clock, a crowd of about six hundred people were seen coming down the road from *Non Pareil*. They were led by a man with a red flag. A few hundred yards before the factory entrance, the crowd swung off the road and started towards the one weak spot – a sixty foot wide gap in the high wire fence where the punts were brought in and unloaded. In front of the gap there was a twenty foot wide trench but the water was only four foot deep and the crowd began wading through.

Here were two armed constables and as the crowd advanced they began to throw bricks and missiles. One man shouted out, 'Dem can't shoot, and if dem shoot, dem can only shoot two ahwee (two of us) and the governor got to come and read the riot act'. Earlier in the day the crowd had taunted the police by saying, 'You Police can't shoot until you read the riot act' and it seems extremely probable that this is what they had, quite incorrectly, been told at their political meetings.

The armed policemen struck by missiles turned and ran. At this moment Corporal James came running up with 2 constables. By this time about 200 people had entered the factory but James shouted to his men 'Let's get them out, don't run from them'. They put their rifles at high port. He and three constables pushed the crowd back into a narrow passage between two bonded stores. In a confined space the police had the advantage but once outside the crowd could attack them

Gathering Strength

from the sides. James was hit and slipped, falling down a trench, in a moment the strikers were on him, de Groot, a constable, went to his help but tripped on a guy-rope and his rifle was snatched away. The man aimed it at him, but could not fire it, he then tried to bayonet de Groot but de Groot managed to grab the rifle and wrest it from him.

At this moment, James decided that they were overwhelmed, he was still on the ground being attacked and ordered his men to fire.

So much makes sense. But from there on, it is obvious that the report was a determined effort to whitewash the police action. The Commission of Inquiry was composed of three Guyanese Civil Servants, one of them wished to issue a minority report and only after much persuasion and after the report had been re-written in its present form did he agree to sign it.

As it stands, the police admit to firing, or having had stolen from them in the scuffles, only 16 bullets. And only four of them admitted to either firing or losing any bullets – and those that did fire claimed that they had shot at the legs of the crowd.

The five people killed had been hit by at least 10 bullets, another bullet was found in a stable and at least 12 to 15 people had been wounded.

As the report said, '. . . we have tried to find the *smallest* number of bullets responsible for the infliction of these several injuries'. They never did decide what the smallest number was, but spoke hopefully of richochets and the possibility that these could make a clean entry wound. They discounted evidence that there had been 'much more firing'.

What seems to have happened is that the crowd, certain that it could not be fired on, had been over-confident. When the firing started it turned and ran and the police, bruised and frightened, decided they were not going to wait for them to regather their confidence so shot them as they ran.

The doctor who gave evidence suggested that one man (Pooran) might have been on all fours when hit as the bullet entered his buttocks and came out of his stomach leaving part of the small intestines protruding. But at cross-examination he admitted the man could have been climbing over a fence. One witness said it was Pooran who was the man that had snatched away de Groot's rifle, another witness said that he had seen the police shoot him as he clambered over the fence and caught his shirt in the barbed wire. But the Commission, while stating there was 'a piece of shirt' on the wire, again discounted the evidence, without commenting on whether the torn piece of cloth matched a tear in Pooran's shirt.

But even before all this came out, everyone knew that at least four people had been killed and a number of others wounded. At such moments, sympathy does not go to a few policemen overwhelmed by a threatening crowd, nor does it look back and wonder who incited the mob, nor who told them that they would not be fired on 'unless the Governor read the riot act'.

Cheddi and Janet Jagan saw in these events the means to publicize and change the sugar workers' conditions and to build up the G.I.W.U. as the people's union.

They organized a funeral march from Enmore to Georgetown and some 7,000 sugar workers joined in the sixteen mile procession. They planned to hold massive demonstrations in the capital afterwards. The Governor forestalled this by declaring Georgetown a proclaimed area, so the funeral procession as it marched into the town to the cemetery was faced at every street by armed police to ensure that they kept on the route.

After the funeral, a special train had been laid on to supplement the ordinary afternoon train, and the procession was led back to the station and dispersed.

But the P.A.C. had achieved a major objective.

Before Enmore, P.A.C. was a movement that could probably rally most of the Indian vote; it could also attract some of the progressive intellectuals of Georgetown, and hoped to get the Negro vote.

After Enmore, Dr and Mrs Jagan were a power in the land. The Indian vote was solidly behind them and they could start to plan for their party. When Burnham came back he was to find that a national leader already existed.

During the period of violence in 1964 Jocelyn Hubbard

Gathering Strength

started a meeting at Enmore by saying, 'Remember we are standing on sacred ground, on hallowed ground, soaked by the blood of martyrs. . . .' Janet Jagan in a private conversation summed it up more succinctly: 'Enmore made us.'

Chapter 12

THE END OF BOOKER'S GUIANA

ENMORE is the point where the course of Guyanese history changed direction. The deaths of the five men were to be of far more than local significance. For the moment, however, those most deeply concerned were P.A.C. and the Commission.

In the P.A.C. *Bulletin* published four days after the riot and one day before the first meeting of the Inquiry Commission there was an article with the headline: 'We asked for Bread . . . They gave us Bullets'. The text was equally strongly worded and, at least subconsciously, the writer was thinking of the beginning of the French Revolution. But when Dr Lachhmansingh, as President of the G.I.W.U., was invited to give evidence he sent a verbal refusal saying that he thought his presence could serve 'no useful purpose'. Dr and Mrs Jagan who had felt strongly enough to lead the procession eleven miles into Georgetown returned the same reply.

It is impossible to believe that they had nothing useful to say. If they boycotted the Commission because they thought it was out to whitewash the event then their action was inexplicable. The hearings were in public and they could have made it extremely difficult for the Commission to keep back facts or evidence that they found embarrassing. One is led to suppose that there were questions the Commission could have asked that would have been extremely awkward for them to have to answer: for instance, who was the mysterious David Alfred?

The Commission itself, for all its carefully mixed conjectures, did find that the workers had a 'real grievance' and

PLATE I

top right:
Mr Forbes Burnham, Q.C.,
Prime Minister and leader of the
People's National Congress Party.

centre right:
Dr Cheddi Jagan, leader of the
People's Progressive Party, now in
opposition.

below right:
Mr Peter d'Aguiar, Minister of
Finance and leader of the
United Force.

below left:
A typical moment of respite:
the demonstrators have become
spectators and stand watching a
tear-gas shell burn harmlessly
in the street. For the moment all
passion is spent until they tire
of watching.

LEFT: PLATE II

top:
Memories of the British raj: the Law Courts, with Queen Victoria majestically looking across at the commercial centre of Georgetown.

centre:
The Public Buildings. The room at the top left is the House of Assembly, the wing to the right is the Prime Minister's office, the rest of the building is occupied by government offices.

bottom:
Stabroek Market, the site of the earliest town the Dutch founded.

PLATE III

Above right: The Riot Squad arrive with tear gas, rifles and loudspeakers.

Below: 'Peaceful pickets' lie down in front of the Public Buildings, the beginning of a day of turmoil.

PLATE IV

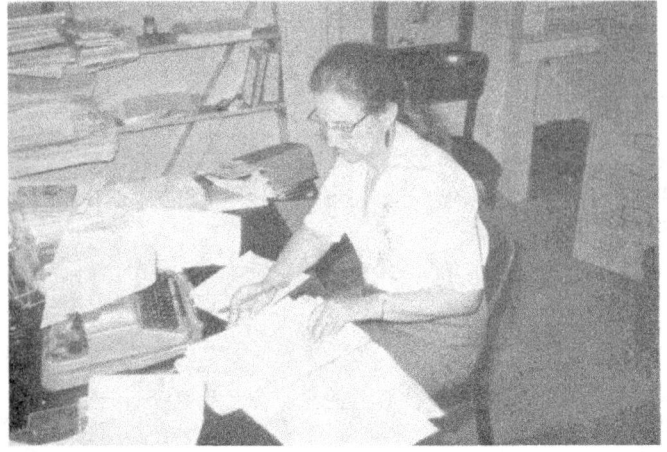

Mrs Janet Jagan, General Secretary of the P.P.P. in her office at Freedom House, the party headquarters.

Freedom House, the scene of many riots and one bomb attack.

Dr Jagan greets two 'Freedom Marchers'. Behind, in white shirt and spectacles, Jocelyn Hubbard smiles happily.

of the police it admitted that '. . . the evidence has established that after the first few shots there was firing which went beyond the requirements of the situation.'

Enmore had lifted the lid off the colony's affairs and the British Government did not like what it saw there. It was obviously time that something was done about it at last.

On July 27th it was announced that a Commission under J. A. Venn, President of Queens' College, Cambridge, would be sent out to inquire into the conditions of the sugar workers. Venn's report left no one in any doubt that the sugar workers were extremely badly treated and that malpractices flourished. Although Dr Jagan and Dr Lachhmansingh had not helped the Inquiry Commission, they both gave evidence before the Venn Commission whose brief concerned working and living conditions in general and was not directly concerned with Enmore.

The report was published almost a year later on July 9, 1949, but there appears to be no reference to it in P.A.C. *Bulletin* until December and then again in January (by which time the *Bulletin* had become *Thunder*), when it is remarked, 'Among the 44 recommendations of the Venn Commission are none for basic changes in the sugar industry'. But this comment was mere political barracking for when the P.P.P. issued its election manifesto in 1953, it said the Party would do its utmost to secure speedier implementation of the Factories Ordinance 'and as far as possible all the recommendations of the Venn Commission affecting Sugar Estate Workers'. These, so far as the Manifesto was concerned, were all the ideas they had for the sugar workers.

Towards the end of 1949 Forbes Burnham returned and it was time to start the popular party of which he would be Chairman in fulfilment of the promise to the British Communist Party. The date chosen was January 1, 1950. P.A.C. Bulletin had served its purpose – but the last two issues, the 42nd and 43rd had the honour of being printed instead of duplicated. Then it was superseded by *Thunder*: Organ of the People's Progressive Party.

Trouble in Guyana

On its masthead it carried the quotation:

Hark the rolling of the Thunder
Lo! the sun And lo there under
Riseth wrath, and hope and wonder.

William Morris and the People's Progressive Party may seem an incongruous mixture of ancient and modern, but it accurately reflected feelings within the new Party. There were those who believed that it should declare itself as Communist, sacrificing immediate benefits for more substantial and lasting gains in the future; there were those who favoured a national liberation front party bringing in anyone who subscribed to independence; and those with more moderate or even rightwing views who thought that having been carried to power by the Jagans they could then dominate or drop them. It was those who believed in consolidating their position as a national front movement who won the day.

The first Party Congress was held fifteen months later, on April 1, 1951. It then adopted a Constitution that, except for minor variations, has continued to the present. The *History of the P.P.P.* points out quite correctly that this was quite new to British Guiana, 'as no mass organization had ever fulfilled such an extensive procedural arrangement for any length of time. The democratic centralism of the P.P.P. has been, unchanged . . . since 1950.'

It is true that the P.P.P. had written into its Constitution the mechanics of a strong centrally dominated party machinery – it did not then, nor has it since, made full use of its potential.

The strongest, *de facto*, position is the General Secretary's – a position that Janet Jagan has held throughout the Party's history. People who are now members of Burnham's party say that this was no Machiavellian trick on her part to ensure that she maintained control. When the Party was formed R. B. O. Hart wanted to be Leader and when he was refused this was offered the General Secretaryship; this he turned down. The struggle was for the high sounding positions and the Secretary post was kicked around, each trying to avoid it because of the work it entailed. The meetings used to take place at the Jagan's house, most of the papers were kept there and, as Janet Jagan did most of the paper work anyway, she was asked to take the post. Whether, in fact, this is really what happened, or whether the Jagans succeeded perfectly in being forced to accept a post they had already decided to hold, cannot now be known – but Janet, armed with the position of General Secretary and the editorship of *Thunder*, was to remain at the centre point of the party, and so was given the power to declare illegal any activity that she did not like, or had not been informed about.

Around the General Secretary is the Party Executive, which consists of seven or eight members including the Chairman, two vice-Chairmen, the Leader and Treasurer who are the real policy making body. When they are joined, at least once a month, by seven members from the General Council they become the Executive Committee whose *imprimatur* can pass any policy that does not directly contravene the Constitution.

This is the 'democratic centralism' – at the heart of the Party. From the General Secretary run the co-ordinating lines to organize and maintain mass support. These pass first to the Constituency Committees, and through them down to the smallest unit, the Party Group. Each Party Group must have at least twelve members and its own Chairman, Secretary and Treasurer. It keeps accounts and minutes and these have to be forwarded to Party H.Q. through the Constituency Committees.

Nominations for the Constituency Committees and the Party Groups have to be vetted by the Party Executive, or at least the General Secretary, before they are recognized.

The P.P.P. has, since 1953, had a reputation for being a highly organized and efficient machine. In fact this has never been true. The working of both the Constituency Committees and the Party Groups has always been spasmodic, depending on the personalities of those in control.

In a country where many people find writing laborious, the Secretaries of Party Groups, and even of the Committees, often found it easier when they had problems to wait until either they or a friend was going to Georgetown. The problem could then be raised verbally with the General Secretary. This development was allowed to continue and not only weakened the chain of command but also led to much waste of time as people brought in verbal reports and asked for advice.

The P.P.P. later learnt how to get the voters to the polls, but it was always the personality of its leaders, and not the party machine, that got them to vote the way the P.P.P. wanted.

As well as trying to build up its party at home, the P.P.P. tried to increase its reputation abroad. Cheddi Jagan spent five months in the summer of 1951 visiting a number of Eastern European countries and by public speeches, broadcasts and articles he denounced British imperialism, praised the Socialist countries, and called for support from their unions, youth leagues and other organizations. The Robertson Commission that took evidence in 1954 came to the conclusion that Dr Jagan only became a convinced communist during this visit to Europe. It, however, gave no reasons for this conclusion.

The 1947 Constitution had been an anachronism even before it was introduced and after the awful disclosures of the Venn Commission the British Government thought it should start as soon as possible on the drawing up of a new Constitution that would be several steps nearer to independence. If they hoped that by making an early start they would stop the political pot from boiling over they made a very great mistake. They sent Sir John Waddington, a former Acting Governor of British Guiana, out as the head of a Constitutional Commission at the end of 1950. The report was published in October 1951 and, as the next elections were not due until April 1953, it meant that campaigning was spread over a year and a half with each party trying to be more radical or nationalistic than any other. It was a certain way to keep politics at boiling point until the day the people went to the polls.

As well, had anyone thought deeply, they would have realized that nothing short of immediate and complete independence would have satisfied any left-wing party. By starting early, they allowed the politicians plenty of time to

The End of Booker's Guiana

tell the people how they were being swindled out of their birthright.

Sir John Waddington must have realised this when he started the hearings. The P.P.P. under the Chairmanship of Burnham argued that the people of Guyana should be allowed to hold their own constituent assembly and all the Waddington Commission had to do was to recommend universal adult suffrage to elect this body.

If the Commission would not let the Guyanese write their own Constitution, then the P.P.P. wanted a single chamber Legislative Assembly of wholly elected members. Over that, but directly responsible to it, there should be an Executive, the equivalent of a Cabinet. The Governor, they said, should have a position similar to a constitutional monarch, with reserved powers only in defence and external affairs.

Any 'checks or balances', either by having a second chamber or by the Governor nominating members, the P.P.P. viewed as both 'unnecessary and offensive'.

In its recommendations the Commission divided. Sir John Waddington favoured a uni-cameral legislative body with checks imposed by a nominated element that in effect would act like an upper house.

Professor V. Harlow and Dr Rita Hinden thought that constitutionally this was a dead-end, that one day the colony would have to have a bi-cameral legislature, and that this could hardly be added later when the nominated members were no longer necessary.

Briefly, the constitutional changes finally decided on by the Colonial Office were:-

a.) Universal adult suffrage.
b.) No property qualifications for those standing for election.
c.) A House of Assembly of 24 elected members and three *ex-officio* (the Chief Secretary, the Attorney General and the Financial Secretary). The Governor was to appoint an independent Speaker, since it was thought that with only 24 elected members the balance of voting might be upset if one party had to give up a member.

d.) A State Council, as an Upper House, comprising nine members, seven appointed by the Governor and two on the advice of the Ministers.

e.) The main policy forming body would be the Executive Council, with the Governor as President, the three ex-officio members, six Ministers with portfolios chosen by the House of Assembly, and a member of State Council, who would rank as Minister without portfolio.

The Robertson Commission was to report that 'from the time it became known that the next elections would be held on a basis of universal adult suffrage the P.P.P. leaders were extremely confident, even cocky, about the outcome'. Nothing that any of the P.P.P. leaders have since said in private conversation lends any justification to this statement. They expected to be the largest minority party faced by a coalition of rightwing parties. They thought that they would have to fight for survival throughout the life of the parliament.

The innumerable checks and balances that had been incorporated, therefore seemed to them repugnant in the highest degree and they criticised the constitution bitterly and consistently right up to the election day. This was certainly to influence their outlook and judgement when they won a landslide victory.

There was much to be criticised in the constitution. *The Times Review of the British Colonies* (Winter 1951) pointed out, '. . . the proposed new Constitution for British Guiana is deliberately drafted to ignore the main political factor in the country, the fact that the East Indian population is now the single largest racial group and will out-number all the groups put together in ten years time'.

In its Winter issue the next year in an article headed, 'British Guiana Politics: Prospects for the Coming Elections' it again emphasised the racial problem by commenting that in the 1947 elections the struggle had appeared to be between the Labour Party, which was predominantly Negro, and the M.P.C.A., which was Indian. The leaders of both these parties had since retired from politics and their parties had disintegrated. No party groupings had developed in the Legislative Council and policy had rested with the Governor. From this it followed that no party would enter the election with any history of achievements. Except, that is, the P.P.P. for whom the June 1948 sugar riots had provided the 'necessary impetus'. In reality, therefore, there was only one political party in Guyana and that was the P.P.P.

But although *The Times* correspondent saw this, nobody else did. The constitution had been framed on the premise that there would be a number of small parties elected, that the Ministers would be selected from whichever group formed the strongest coalition, and that the temporary parliamentary alliances would gradually coalesce and form a two-party system.

It is difficult to understand how, having taken the responsibility for framing a constitution, the Colonial Office did not see that it had a responsibility for ensuring that it worked and, at least by advice and consultation, encouraged the formation of a limited number of parties so that the vote would not be hopelessly split.

As it was, there were 24 seats and for these 130 candidates offered themselves. The P.P.P. had put up 22 candidates. Their only major opponent, the National Democratic Party (N.D.P.) put up fourteen, having split just before the election, and a runaway faction, the People's National Party, put up eight candidates, some of them against the N.D.P. There were two other small parties, the United Guiana Party and the United Farmers' and Workers' Party, who put up seven candidates.

For the rest there were the unbelievable number of seventy-nine independents. In Western Berbice constituency alone, the voters had the choice of 13 different candidates!

When the counting was over out of the 208,000 voters, 152,000 valid votes had been cast and the P.P.P. held 51%. Much was to be made of the fact that a party supported by only 37% of the potential electorate was to hold 75% of the seats, 18 out of the 24. Seventy-eight candidates lost their deposits.

Trouble in Guyana

But there were a number of significant points in the election.

It was the first election under universal suffrage and it was to prove to have had one of the lowest turn-out of voters. Between 85% and up to 95% is now accepted as usual in a Guyanese general election. One reason for this was that the P.P.P. still had not organized itself, but certainly was far superior to every other party. Had there been other properly organized parties, more people might have been encouraged to vote. The Colonial Office had no one else but itself to blame if 51% of those who took the trouble to vote, voted P.P.P.

The Times correspondent had touched on the main point when he foresaw the P.P.P. as the only vital political force. For one thing it represented through its two leaders, Jagan and Burnham, both the major races. For another, it was the only party that had a clear cut nationalistic programme with a reputation behind it of actively working for its beliefs, both in the Legislative Council and in public demonstrations and meetings. All other parties were merely a pale reflection of what the P.P.P. promised and had already achieved.

The Colonial Office was now faced by a party that held 18 seats in the House of Assembly and would therefore put up all the six Ministers in the Executive Council, the main policy forming body, where it would then have a clear majority. In the State Council, it was admittedly in a minority, but under the Constitution, had the State Council tried to delay any important bill, the P.P.P. could have called for a joint session and would again have possessed a clear majority.

The checks and balances of the new constitution had gone out of the window; except for such reserved powers as the Governor possessed, the P.P.P. were in complete command and the colony was theirs.

Chapter 13

A PROMISE TO REDEEM?

On April 27, 1953, the electorate went to the polls and returned the P.P.P. It was a widely popular result and a gigantic meeting was held at Bourda Green in Georgetown to celebrate. All the Party leaders stood up and said a few words. They presented a united and victorious front and nobody can remember what anyone said except for the opening remarks of Janet Jagan. When it came to her turn, she started her speech by saying, 'In 1946 I gave birth to a baby and tonight I have seen it grown into maturity'. For those that did not see eye to eye with the Jagans these were ominous words; it seemed as though Janet thought of them as part of 'her baby' and they did not like this.

Outwardly the Party joined in the widespread rejoicing at their victory, but in their inner councils victory brought them to the edge of disintegration.

In *Forbidden Freedom*, Cheddi Jagan has said that they expected to win only five, at the most seven, seats. Even up to the night of the polls, the Party had planned its strategy for that of the largest party *in opposition*. Only Rory Westmaas, then a Communist, argued that they would win seventeen seats.

While the P.P.P. was a party in the making, the differences of opinion had been glossed over. But once the party won power it was obvious that the final arbitrator for rewards would be the leader, Dr Jagan. Past services might well appear less important than conformity to the party line.

There was, for instance, the help that Dr Lachhmansingh had given to Dr Jagan. Dr Jagan had chosen the Corentyne

Coast as his constituency, with its large number of Indian sugar workers, only to find that he was being contested by a Dr Leon Sharples who had lived there for years and had by unselfish generosity won an apparently unshakeable majority. It was Lachhmansingh with an earthy, no bones about it speech, who asked them whether they were voting for the free medicines they'd been given or for the Party that had fought for them from Enmore onwards. Was Lachhmansingh just a part of Janet's Party?

But the real cause of the trouble was the promise that had been made to Burnham, implied or direct, that he would lead the Party.

At the annual Party Congress held in the February before the elections, Janet Jagan had had the motion passed that Cheddi Jagan should be the Leader of the Legislative Group*. At the time, Cheddi Jagan was the only member of the party in the Legislature, so there seemed to be little harm in allowing him to be his own Leader. As well, the P.P.P. constitution clearly stated in paragraph 8, 'The Officers of the Party shall be the Chairman, First and Second vice-Chairman, *the Leader of the Legislative Group, with status next to the Chairman, the General Secretary...*'. The situation had now changed radically. The colony's Constitution stated that the *majority* party should elect a Leader of the House. Who else should this be, argued Burnham, but the Chairman and 'Leader' of the Party. But Janet Jagan as General Secretary argued that Dr Jagan as Leader of the Legislative Group must obviously be the 'Leader of the House'.

On Sunday May 3rd the General Council met to decide whom should be given Ministerial posts and the recommendations for portfolios that they would make to the Governor.

A meeting with the Governor had been arranged for the next morning. It should have been a pleasant morning for most while the spoils of victory were divided. Instead, no decision could be reached, and another meeting had to be arranged for that evening which continued until the early hours of the morning.

*Burnham must have felt quite safe at letting this motion pass especially as the P.P.P. did not expect to win an outright majority.

A Promise to Redeem?

The meeting with the Governor had to be postponed for 24 hours and in the afternoon another Council meeting was held. During this meeting, Clinton Wong, Senior vice-Chairman, said he would resign. He did not make his resignation public until Sunday May 17th but in a letter he then published he said he had given up his post because 'It is obvious that since the last Annual Party Conference in February last, a newly elected, irresponsible and unmanageable element has been able to direct the Party's affairs by means of having the greatest voting strength both in the Party's Executive and General Council'. Clinton Wong said he would remain in the party but would not hold office.

Already there were rumours of dissension in the newspapers and the Governor's meeting could not be postponed again. There was nothing else for Burnham to do but to accept, momentarily, the majority ruling.

At two minutes past ten the next morning the Governor saw Burnham and Jagan in a meeting that lasted until 11.45 a.m. They strolled in the garden outside for press photographers. It was announced that Jagan was Leader of the Legislative Group (not, however, of the House) and Burnham was reported 'from sources within the party' to have agreed to give up his 'lucrative' law practice and accept a portfolio. The 'sources' said that he had also accepted Jagan as Leader of the Party. The Burnhamite opinion was that on this, and on a number of future occasions, the 'sources' were none other than Janet Jagan whose careful indiscretions put Burnham in the difficult position of either denying that he had agreed to such conditions, and so admitting there was a split, or else ignoring the leak. He chose the latter.

As well, the 'sources' said the portfolios were probably going to:–

Agriculture	Jagan
Education	Burnham
Labour	Ashton Chase
Works	Sidney King
Health	Dr Lachhmansingh
Local Government	Janet Jagan

This too was felt to be half sweetness to those 'said' to be in and half threat to those 'said' to be left out.

Until the leak to the press, Burnham's photograph had always taken precedence in the newspapers usually followed by Janet Jagan's. Cheddi Jagan's had appeared sometimes before, sometimes after, other members. From that moment, it was Cheddi Jagan's that was most prominent and Burnham's that was haphazardly placed.

But the announcement after the meeting with the Governor was only a momentary truce and there were other deeper problems unsolved. As Sidney King was later to say the Party was 'nothing but a broad democratic alliance against Imperialism'. It had expected to be a minority and had gone to the elections not as a disciplined Communist party but as a national front movement. It had post-dated its struggle to the future, although in its first party elections the Jaganite left-wing had ensured that it held the commanding positions.

The disagreement with Burnham brought this problem out into the open. Those who had joined what they thought was a left-wing movement based on nationalistic ideals, had thought they could always disown or get rid of the 'extremists' later. They now found that it was the 'extremists' who held control of the party.

The dilemma was obvious. At the very moment of victory, they were faced with the showdown that they, as well as the progressive side, had thought would come later. Clinton Wong represented this position. They had either to give up hopes of office, or accept the extremists – worse still the issue was not really over ideological differences, but over whether Burnham or Jagan should lead them. And both then appeared to be far to the left.

The battle within the party continued. On Friday May 8th, a fourth meeting of the General Council was held and again resulted in deadlock. Janet Jagan, as General Secretary, issued a press statement with, she said, the agreement of Burnham and the Council, announcing that there was disagreement over whether the term Leader of the Legislative Group was 'synonymous' with Leader of the House. She said that on Sunday, Burnham and Chase had refused to accept

A Promise to Redeem?

ministries, at the Monday meeting there had been no decision but on Friday the Council had ruled that the terms were synonymous. She went on to say that the Friday meeting broke up with Burnham, Chase and Van Sertima saying that they would not accept portfolios. It was decided that the distributtion of portfolios should be deferred to the next day, Saturday. She obviously believed that there was wider popular support for Jagan than Burnham, and to strengthen her hand had made the issue public.

Burnham, therefore, had to try and mobilize his supporters. An attempt was made to hold a public meeting. But a car toured Georgetown advising the Progressive Youth Movement not to attend. Janet Jagan, again speaking as General Secretary, had it announced over the wireless that she had not authorized any public meeting.

The fifth General Council meeting took place on Saturday and no decision was reached. But at the sixth meeting on Sunday May 10th, Burnham and Chase finally gave way and agreed to accept Ministerial posts.

It was agreed that the allocation of Ministries as earlier announced would stand with the exception that Jai Naraine Singh would be Minister for Local Government and Janet Jagan would instead stand for Deputy Speaker.

This was no concession on the part of Mrs Jagan but the sensible decision that her time would now be best occupied in pulling together the discordant elements in the party.

When the secret ballot took place in the House of Assembly for the Deputy Speaker, it is interesting that there were 17 votes for Janet (so at least one of the P.P.P. failed to vote for her), three for Burnham's sister, Jessie Burnham, two for Clinton Wong, one person did not vote, and another vote was spoilt. In other words the opposition made no attempts to vote for their own members, knowing that was hopeless but tried to add to any split that existed in the P.P.P.

In the very moment of its success the party had almost foundered. This may explain much that followed, which up to now has seemed inexplicable. One has only to look at the allocation of portfolios to see how serious the split was.

The Ministers were divided into three: Dr Jagan and

Sidney King formed one group loyal to the General Secretary. Burnham and Chase formed another. While Lachhmansingh and Jai Naraine Singh were both individualists, the former was later to join with Burnham in an attempt to capture the P.P.P. and the latter eventually became a one man party.

The Burnham/Jagan split was to have far more serious consequences than merely taking away the Negro vote from the P.P.P. One member of the Party of those days says that he had never seen two men work so closely together. He remembers how in the Executive meetings Cheddi Jagan having laid out the different aspects of a problem as he saw them would say, in all sincerity, 'No doubt the Chairman will enlighten us. . . '. Burnham was, or could have been, the brains of the party.

When Burnham eventually left he took with him nearly all the intellectuals, except for Keith and Martin Carter and Rory Westmaas, who then believed that the P.P.P. should be a Communist Party – later they were to be vilified and expelled as leftist-deviationists.

But the immediate effects were even worse. The P.P.P. had learnt from its camgaigning that highly radical views paid off. But once Burnham and Jagan no longer worked as a united command there was no one to decide on the course of events. Instead, the Party became a group of individuals, all looking to the next elections, and each trying to show himself as the true leader of the left wing.

The National Front as an objective had ceased to exist even before the P.P.P. officially took office and those moderates who remained did so because of the rewards of office – or the hope of one day picking up the bits that were left.

The tragedy for Guyana was that politics were now bound to follow racial lines.

Chapter 14

THE PRICE THAT WAS PAID

CHEDDI JAGAN was now firmly in the seat of power. On May 11th, he went to see the Governor alone; six days before he had been accompanied by the Chairman, Mr Burnham. He and the Governor between them discussed the final allotment of portfolios and the opening of the House of Assembly.

The revolt spluttered on for a day or two. Seventy-eight members of Clinton Wong's Constituency signed a letter to the General Secretary asking her to explain the stories of the 'Red Menace' that was said to exist in the Party. The General Secretary replied saying she would answer when she had taken it up with the General Council.

On May 18th the House of Assembly was sworn in.

The Secret Ballot for Deputy Speaker had shown that one P.P.P. member voted against Janet. When it came to voting for the six Ministers, Burnham obtained 19 votes while the other five only won 18 each, proving that one of the minority party had voted for him – technically he had more support in the House than Jagan, but Jagan, as agreed, became Leader of the House.

Once in office, all the problems of running departments, helping constituents, speaking in the Assembly and formulating party policy began to tell on the inexperienced new Ministers. To begin with the Waddington Constitution created a great many changes in Govermental procedure but not all of these had been ironed out by the time the new Ministers took office.

The Waddington Constitution was not so advanced as it might have been but for British Guiana it did represent a major shift in the political balance. Until then all correspondence had gone automatically to the Chief Secretary's Office and from there it had been distributed to different departments. With ministerial government this obviously had to be changed and the setting up of ministerial registries took a month to complete.

When later the P.P.P. Government was said in a British White Paper to have been inefficient and large arrears of work were found on the Ministers' desks, Ashton Chase, in his book *133 Days*, denied this and blamed it on the slowness of the change-over. Unfortunately for his argument a letter was subsequently found on the Government files written by Mr King (Minister for Communications and Works) to the Chief Secretary thanking him for the speed with which the change-over had been made.

The Governor was far nearer to understanding the magnitude of the change-over than the P.P.P. Chase says that soon after the Government was formed Sir Alfred Savage told them that 'We would have to go around the country and see things for ourselves so as to be able to better administer our departments. He anticipated that it would take us three or four months before anything would start to come out of our offices.'

But this advice did not suit the Ministers. They probably did not realize it consciously, because it was not until 1962 that one of them began to exploit the method effectively, but what they wanted to create was a pork-barrel government.

This is brought out clearly in the last chapter of Chase's book, headed *Important Qualitative Changes*, where he says,

'In the day considerable time was spent interviewing callers to the Ministerial Building. On the average, every day we shared some 200 callers between us. We thought at first that this was because of the recency of the Ministerial system. Rather than the number reducing, however, they grew daily . . . it was because of the ready relief which people were getting from the Ministers and which spread far and wide that these callers became more frequent. Something was being done, and done quickly.'

The Price that was Paid

This better than anything else describes how and why the P.P.P. government fell. There were only six Ministers. On an average, therefore, each Minister saw over thirty people each day. If one allows ten minutes as the very shortest possible interview, and many must have taken twice or three times as long, they were spending five to seven hours of their working day dealing with personal problems. On top of this they had their paper work to do, their policy planning, their discussions with their Civil Servants, their party meetings, their work in the House of Assembly (when it was in session) and such social functions as they thought it their duty to attend.

If this were not enough Janet Jagan, as General Secretary, in the first few weeks demanded that each day the Ministers should come to the Jagan's house to discuss their work and obtain Party agreement for their activities. However, Burnham refused to attend these meetings and they were soon allowed to lapse.

No government could hope to work giving so much time to individuals and so little to the government of the country as a whole. Chase's *Qualitative Change* could only be for the worse. Added to these difficulties caused by inexperience and overwork were the equivocal positions the Ministers assumed. They seemed uncertain of the roles they had set themselves to play.

In the May issue of *Thunder* Sidney King, then extremely left wing, wrote that the P.P.P. was not the Government but as the 'Peoples Opposition has moved into positions of strategic advantage in the House of Assembly and in the Executive Council'. That this was no personal deviation in dialectic thought is shown by Mr Ramkarran on June 18th saying in the House, 'I can assure you, Sir, that we will do our best, as the Opposition Party, to carry out the wishes of the People'. At this point the Attorney General, with commendable desire to see fair play and keep the record straight, interrupted Ramkarran to say that he could not quite see how the majority could be the 'opposition' and felt that hon. Member was possibly getting muddled. But Ramkarran denied that he had made any mistake and ploughed on with his speech.

Psychologically it suited the different factions in the P.P.P.

Trouble in Guyana

to believe that they were in opposition. To them as individuals it represented not what it claimed as a group, the opposition of Socialism to a Capitalistic Constitution, but the opposition of the different groups to the events that were taking place for which none of them at the next election wished to accept full responsibility. Only the next election would prove who were the true party and who the deviationists.

It was in this atmosphere that they set about consolidating their own groups – and, at the same time, running their Government into the ground.

To read Hansard is to find one example of equivocation and defiance following another.

The first business session received messages from the Queen, the Colonial Secretary and the Governor. Dr Jagan proposed a motion on the reply to the Governor. After some time the Attorney General suggested that it would be more correct if they started on the Loyal Address to the Queen first. There was no move from the P.P.P. bench and the Opposition leader, Mr Kendall, proposed it and was seconded by an independent.

The Speaker asked if anyone then wished to speak on the motion. Again there was silence from the P.P.P. and he said that he understood therefore that the motion was passed. Again silence.

It is impossible to see what was gained by a majority party that claimed it wished to stay within the Commonwealth behaving in this manner. A little more subtlety and forethought and they could probably have used the Loyal Address to their advantage.

Reading Hansard is to meet again and again the buzz of an angry mosquito that never quite settles and stings. On the same day that Ramkarran spoke of his party being in opposition, Mr Adjoha Singh started his speech, 'Mr Speaker, hon. Members, hon. Comrades.'

MR SPEAKER: I cannot allow that reference. I have never heard it before in the Legislature.

MR SINGH: . . . Today we have a People's Government. . . .

The Price that was Paid

It was all rather puposeless and Janet Jagan took leave and went off to Copenhagen to affiliate her newly formed Women's Progressive Organization to the Women's International Democratic Federation where she was elected to the Congress Presidium. Instead of celebrating the P.P.P. victory, she had instead cried for the moon, 'we need guidance and help . . . We in the Colonial world are tied economically and politically like slaves of old . . . Help us to win freedom for all the oppressed colonial peoples of the world.'

Afterwards she went to Roumania – there seemed to be so much time before one had to face reality. As well, it was essential to see that the Socialist countries were on the side of her husband, and not Burnham.

But things were moving on. On July 24th a motion was put forward to repeal the Undesirable Publications (Prohibition of Importation) Bill. A subject that had already achieved some notoriety.

The proposer was Burnham and it was his maiden speech. It was significant that he had waited so long before speaking.

The bill had first been proposed in March 1952 by Mr Lionel Luckhoo, President of the M.P.C.A., as an attempt to stop the importation of Communist literature, which by then according to Janet Jagan had reached about half a million copies. Mr Luckhoo's proposal did for Communist literature what the case against Penguin Books later achieved for *Lady Chatterley's Lover*. It also prevented him, and those associated with him, from winning the 1953 election as he then seemed to be firmly identified with the old order.

The Bill did not become an Ordinance until February 1953 and was never applied. Nearly everyone was against it and even the Archbishop of the West Indies came out strongly in support of its repeal and a return to the right to read what one wished.

But the P.P.P. were not satisfied with merely repealing the bill. In 1952 Dr Jagan had brought into the colony, without declaring them, 222 copies of *Soviet Literature* and 534 copies of *Soviet Women* in a consignment of books and gramophone records. Even the most hardened smuggler would, one would have thought, have hesitated about this. The Customs confiscated them and on October 6, 1952 burnt them, without, as the P.P.P. had hoped, putting them up for sale. Dr Jagan thought he had lost about £100.

Dr Jagan had appealed against the action by the Customs but, although the Customs' action appeared to be perfectly legal, the Attorney General in drafting the Ordinance had put in a retroactive clause stating that the action could not be challenged.

When the P.P.P. put forward their Bill to repeal the Ordinance, they also inserted a clause invalidating the previous validation, thereby making it possible to open a case against the Customs. This, for a mere £100 and as Dr Jagan told the House of Assembly to 'prove that every dog has his day' and this was Dr Jagan's day! This display of petty spite cost the support of many who still viewed the P.P.P. as a party whose youthful exuberance made it unpopular with the Governor. It has meant that instead of being passed immediately, the Opposition members in the Assembly opposed it, and the Governor in the Executive Council refused to give it his sanction.

The P.P.P. Ministers tried to have it all ways at once. They publicly spoke of themselves as 'The People's Ministers' and at the same time tried to use the Executive Council, in which they had control, as a rubber stamp to enforce decisions arrived at previously in what they called 'The People's Council': a rather grandiose title for back-room discussions by members of the party.

While denigrating the Constitution, the Ministers tried, under the powers conferred on them by the same Constitution, to write themselves blank cheques. They then complained when the Governor wished to discuss the drafting, the intention and the effect of the proposed legislation before he signed it. They went to great lengths to destroy, for propaganda purposes, any trust the Governor might have given them, and then complained bitterly if he did not give them any powers they asked for.

The Rice Farmers' Security of Tenure Bill was a typical example. Many landowners were not giving their tenants the

The Price that was Paid

services they legally had to provide. All were agreed that a new Bill was necessary, but when the P.P.P. put up its Bill it made use of powers that dated back to the eighteenth century when the colony was under Dutch rule. It incorporated the right for District Commissioners at their own discretion to undertake work that the landlord had not done and to make him liable for the charges. A case for this alone might be argued, but they then gave the District Commissioner the right of *parate execution* which meant that the Commissioner could sell up any landlord who did not *immediately* make payment. To the Governor and others it appeared as though the P.P.P. were exhuming long dead forms of legislation to give themselves the power to dispossess any individual landowner they did not like.

Dr Jagan, although Leader of the House, also remained President of the Sawmill and Forest Workers Union. Dr Lachhmansingh (Minister of Health) was President of G.I.W.U., the other ministers also held onto their trade union posts. And during all this time of Legislation and P.P.P. administration stoppages of work or strikes were on the increase, encouraged by the inflammatory speeches made by those in power who claimed that they were in opposition.

They tried to annul a Trades Dispute Ordinance passed in wartime; this was acceptable except that they wished to stop such essential services as water, electricity, and the fire brigade from being legally bound to give ten days' notice of a strike to allow time for arbitration. The P.P.P. did not wish this clause to stand in the Bill and in the uncertain conditions it was not surprising that this was one blank cheque the Governor did not wish to sign.

But the crux of the matter came when the P.P.P., still without any firm base or clear understanding of the situation, decided to re-open the fight for the control of the sugar workers unions. As things stood there were still about four years to go before it had to face the electorate and it was still a popular and radical government. It could not, however, leave well alone.

On July 21st, after only seven weeks of effective office, the Minister of Labour wrote to the Sugar Producers' Association

(S.P.A.) and asked whether it would reconsider giving recognition to the G.I.W.U. The S.P.A. replied that it might be possible to accept the G.I.W.U. as the officially recognized union for the fieldworkers, and the M.P.C.A. for the factory workers.

What subsequently happened shows how badly the P.P.P. was split. Dr Lachhmansingh (the Minister for Health and President of the G.I.W.U.) was completely unaware of the real P.P.P. policy. He told the S.P.A. that he would much rather negotiate an agreement with them than fight for one. He then went further and addressing a meeting of sugar workers told them roundly that things had changed since the elections and that now in proposing to strike they were in effect striking against their own government. He told them to be patient and promised that they would be looked after. That evening, when he got home, he was rung up by Janet Jagan and asked whether the report she had been given was true. When he said it was, Janet Jagan is reputed to have told him that if he ever again told the people that the P.P.P. was the government he would be out of his Ministry.

When the next meeting with the S.P.A. took place Sidney King (Minister of Works) arrived uninvited. There was no official reason for the Minister of Works to attend a meeting between employers and union leaders. He was there, in fact, to ensure that the Jagan line went through. Not surprisingly, the meeting broke up without any decisions being reached on either side, and a strike was called for the next day, August 31st.

Within ten days all the estates had come out and an estimated 1,900 tons of cane that had already been burnt was left standing in the fields, or lying in the unmanned punts. The loss to the colony was about £80,500.

A *New Statesman and Nation* correspondent wrote, 'the S.P.A. looked somewhat cynically upon the spectacle of one Minister arbitrating a strike called by another'. He had not realised the full irony, that the Minister (Sidney King) who should have been arbitrating had called the strike, while the Minister (Dr Lachhmansingh) who should, as union leader have called it, would still have preferred to negotiate.

The Price that was Paid

Having successfully brought the sugar industry to a halt, the extremists in the P.P.P. then decided to call for a General Strike, presumably hoping that they would then be in a strong enough position to demand a new Constitution or even independence.

But they had not analysed their position. They no longer had the full support of Burnham, and therefore of the Negro, nor the trade unionists. The electorate had not voted them into power in order to go on strike and could see no reason to turn out into the streets to defend a government that already had all the powers it needed. The extremists brought to bear all the pressure they could, but there was never any chance of the strike going beyond their immediate followers – the Indian field workers.

The General Strike was never more than a fantasy. But, worse still, the sugar strike began to falter and the P.P.P. quickly decided to call it off before it collapsed. They gave up the idea of trying to capture the colony by mass action, or even of holding it to ransom by withdrawing labour from the plantations. Instead they impetuously decided to achieve all their aims at once by using their parliamentary strength. They would legislate their way into control of the unions and so guarantee a General Strike.

On September 15th, they laid before the Executive Council a Labour Relations Bill. Except for a copy that had gone to the Labour Commissioner at 4.30 p.m. the day before, this was the first time that anyone, Governor, employers or union leaders, had seen it.

In the Executive Council the Governor, as President, and the *ex-officio* members objected to it on principle and suggested amendments. The Governor also suggested that before publication it should go to the trade unions and the employers' associations for their comments and suggestions. It may seem strange that a government should, over such an important issue, make public its own views before consultation, thus making it difficult for itself to concede any point without publicly backing down. But this, of course, was the very reason why it was done in this way, not only in 1953 but again in 1963. The more extreme members of the party wanted to make it virtually impossible for the more moderate members to negotiate an agreement.

On September 19th the Bill was published in the Official Gazette and on September 24th the Minister asked leave of the Speaker to move a motion to suspend the Standing Rules and Orders to enable the Bill to be taken through *all its stages* that day. On the same day the G.I.W.U. called off the strike.

The meaning was quite clear. The P.P.P. had shown its power on the estates by calling the strike and was now going to use its voting strength in the Legislature to get its Bill through. The Speaker, however, refused and the P.P.P. staged a walk-out. It was not until October 8th that the Bill came up.

The P.P.P. have relied on the fact that few people would ever see a copy of the Bill, and have tried to cover up their own errors of judgement by pretending that the Bill was a liberal, if not conservative, proposal. Unfortunately for them they became victims of their own propaganda and once again in 1963 were not able to foresee the violent reaction their proposals were bound to create.

The Bill is, in fact, one that only a government could hope to pass if it were in a position of impregnable strength, and its opponents knew that, if necessary, they could find protection from courts that were both rapid and impartial.

In British Guiana in 1953, the P.P.P. had many enemies and these enemies believed that, if the P.P.P. could arm itself with the powers offered by such a Bill, they might well be wiped out before the slow and expensive machinery of justice had declared what was, and what was not, constitutionally *ultra vires*.

They acknowledged that there were a number of liberal clauses but they pointed out that each was subsequently invalidated by the discretionary powers given to the Minister. They claimed that a determined Minister could understand the Bill to mean that:–

any group of people calling themselves a trade union could ask for a ballot among the workers and the Minister on his own authority could direct that the ballot was held;

if the result was not satisfactory to the Minister, he could

The Price that was Paid

go on calling for fresh ballots until the result he wanted turned up. After that there could be no more balloting for at least two years and only then if the Minister wanted it;

the Minister could regulate how the ballot was carried out;

if a trade union he supported won a ballot, he could then issue a certificate making it the officially recognized union for that group of workers;

any employer who refused to recognize this union was liable, on summary conviction, to pay £100 for the first day, and £20 for each subsequent day he failed to recognize it;

if the employer was considered to be an individual, as opposed to a corporation, he could be fined the same amount and also imprisoned for one year.

Neither trade unions nor employers could withstand such powers and when in his book *133 Days* Ashton Chase later wrote, 'It (the Bill) aimed at minimising inter-union rivalry', the TUC agreed with him entirely. They thought it would do more than that, it would cut out all union rivalry as there would only be the P.P.P. unions left in existence.

The Governor by this time agreed with the trade unionists and was convinced of the P.P.P.'s intention to take over the unions. This was one of the deciding factors when the suspension of the Constitution was considered. Although the P.P.P. were able to pass the Bill through the House of Assembly on October 8th, it was, in fact, an idle gesture indulged in by them to keep their minds off far more important events.

On Sunday October 4th, the Secretary of State for Colonial Affairs had joined a Privy Council Meeting at Balmoral where the Queen was residing. The decision was taken that P.P.P. misrule must come to an end. British troops and ships were to be sent to support the Governor when he made his announcement that the P.P.P. no longer had legitimate power.

The fantasy of a 'People's Government' that was 'in opposition', had come to an end. It was to be a number of years before the P.P.P. could get back to a similar position of strength that they had so recklessly thrown away.

Chapter 15

ANTI-PARTY ACTIVITIES

On Friday October 9th, the Governor by official proclamation declared the Constitution suspended and the P.P.P. Ministers to be devoid of any legal power. Much has been written about the wisdom of this action, but very little attention has been given to *how* it was done.

The method employed suggests two things: that the British Government were both giving the P.P.P. a chance to come to their senses, and were at the same time calling their bluff. In all accounts given in the past, the emphasis has been placed on the use of force – in that British soldiers were sent to Georgetown. But no one has commented on the fact that the British Government did not employ an equally, or even more important weapon – secrecy.

Dr Jagan in *Forbidden Freedom* says that on the morning of Sunday October 4th he was told that there were rumours that British troops were going to be sent to Guyana. As the sugar strike was over and there was no question of a collapse of law and order this could have had only one meaning.

On Monday October 5th, the British press carried details of the Cruiser *Superb* sailing under 'sealed orders' to Jamaica where it had picked up 400 men of the Royal Welch Fusiliers and sailed again 'for an unknown destination'.

The next day the frigate *Bigbury Bay* sailed from Jamaica with 200 more soldiers and, according to *Associated Press*, Caribbean Headquarters 'admitted' that troops were being 'rushed' to British Guiana.

But it was only four days later that the inhabitants of Georgetown awoke to find British troops in the streets. Late

Anti-Party Activities

that evening the Colonial Office announced naval and military forces were being sent to Georgetown 'in order to preserve peace. . . '. They were needed it was said, 'because of the intrigues of Communists and their associates, some in Ministerial posts. . . '.

The British Government was perfectly able to keep secret the movement of a few naval ships and some troops if it had wanted to. If it had really expected trouble would it have given four or five days notice that it was sending them? It seems, to say the least, improbable.

The P.P.P. forewarned that the British were about to take a tough line, if not worse, showed more clearly than ever before how divided was their leadership and how incompetent and muddled was their thinking.

What did they do in all the time they had available?

The answer is virtually nothing. They argued with the Governor in the Executive Council and tried to get the Speaker to let them debate the probable, and actual, arrival of the troops.

Two weeks earlier, when the Speaker had not allowed the Suspension of Standing Rules and Orders to enable the Labour Relations Bill to be taken through all its stages in one afternoon, the P.P.P. had walked out. Now they tamely accepted the ruling that they could not discuss the possible arrival of British troops and spent the last few hours in the House of Assembly putting the Labour bill through its final committee stages.

For 129 days they had played at being a revolutionary government, for the last four days when indeed they might have had some justification for turning their fiery speeches into action, they tried to hide behind the skirts of a Constitution they despised.

They put out a pamphlet headed ON GUARD; it was printed on pink paper but it was true blue in content. The last paragraph starts 'Whatever happens in the next few days let us remain firm and calm. If our leaders are arrested new leaders will spring up. If our country is placed under martial law *let our people stay in their houses and go about their several business in peace. . . .*'

Trouble in Guyana

Three days later they called a General Strike, for two days the sugar workers were out but on the third day they started to go back to work and the General Strike was stillborn. They could no longer bring even the sugar industry to a halt.

It is a waste of time to argue whether the British Government were wise or foolish to suspend the Constitution: certainly, if their aim was to end P.P.P. rule, their method proved signally ineffective and merely confirmed Dr Jagan's position as a national hero.

It is more instructive, and the P.P.P. did not learn from this experience, to analyse what these events show and to see what the P.P.P.'s true position was.

By the electorate they had been given an unassailable majority for the next four years. But they were so rigid in their thinking, so divided in their ambitions, that they could not comprehend what they had gained. Instead they did all they could to undermine their own legal position and took refuge in the childish pretence that they were in 'opposition'. They wasted their time in futile arguments amongst themselves on whether or not a 'progressive government' could come into existence without armed revolt. But they lacked the courage to realise that if this was worth discussing at all, it was of paramount importance and must be settled once and for all, immediately. Thereafter they would have to act as a disciplined party and carry out whatever decisions they might make. Their treating it as a Shibboleth, to test the ideological beliefs of individual members, made them incapable of any concerted action, or any coherent policy.

When, if ever, they should have called for a popular insurrection, they found that they had neither the wish, the means, nor the organization to do so.

Instead they exhorted the people to stay calm and at home. The people in Georgetown were prepared to do the former but they were certainly not going to stay at home.

The day the British troops arrived was the first day of the Inter-colonial Test Match series and they were going to Bourda Cricket Ground. It was worth it, by the end of the day Trinidad had knocked up 237 for 5! That indeed might have been a good day to call a General Strike.

Anti-Party Activities

Subsequently, after house searches and arrests, the British Government found nothing to show any secret connexions or deep laid plans of a Communist take-over. They found what they had suspected, the P.P.P. was crying 'Wolf'. What had been serious was the P.P.P.'s use of strikes and demonstrations as a threat, while it tried to push through legislation that had none of the normal constitutional safeguards. It couldn't have it all ways, but it did have four days before the troops arrived to take a second glance.

It took a quick look and decided its safest bet was political martyrdom – which was, under the circumstances, not such a bad choice – except it had forgotten that the party was split.

When in 1956, Dr Jagan gave an address behind closed doors to the P.P.P. congress, he was to see his party's behaviour in much the same way as described above, saying:

'It is clear from my analysis that in the period of our Party ascendancy up to October 1953 we committed deviations to the left. We definitely over-rated the revolutionary possibilities of our party, the leader of the liberation movement. We allowed our zeal to run away with us; we became swollen-headed, pompous, bombastic. "In order to smash these powerful enemies" said Stalin, "It is necessary to have a flexible and well-considered policy to take advantage of every crack in the enemy camp and skill in finding allies".'

'We were attacking everybody at the same time. We tended towards what Mao Tse Tung called *"all struggle and no unity"*. This is how Comrade Mao Tse Tung attacked the left dogmatists who during the 10 years (1927–1937) civil war period advocated overthrowing everybody. He said, "You cannot overthrow those in power, so you want to overthrow those who are not in power. They are already out of power, yet you still want to overthrow those who are not in power. They are already out of power, yet you still want to overthrow them".'

The Constitution was suspended and the Government was out. Ten days later Burnham and Jagan flew off to London, and though the Labour Party asked the Conservative Government some questions and launched a luke-warm attack, the Labour Party Executive on November 10th, informed all its Constituency Committees that it should not give them support nor let them appear on Labour Party platforms, since, they said, the Labour Executive viewed 'their undermining the Constitution as a matter of profound regret'.

When later they toured India to ask for support, Nehru was careful to see that they travelled under the aegis of the Congress Party and not the Indian government. When they got back in February 1954 they had nothing to show for their journeys.

Meanwhile in Guyana, the split had re-opened. Only four days after Jagan and Burnham had left, Reuters reported from Georgetown,

'Mrs Jagan has staved off for the present a threatened split among leaders of the P.P.P. . . . Moderate wing supporters of L. F. S. Burnham . . . sent Mrs Jagan a letter earlier this week demanding that she call a special meeting of the General Council. Otherwise, they said, they would issue a public statement denouncing extremists in the party . . . Mr Burnham is dissatisfied with his secondary role to Dr Jagan in London. He has been reported as saying that he would never join another party. . . .'

Reuters correspondent went on to say that Janet Jagan had persuaded Ashton Chase and 'other Burnhamite supporters' to drop all action until they had seen how the two got on in England.

The story of British Guiana since 1950 is one of almost annual pilgrimages of one Commission or another to inquire into something that has gone wrong or ought to be put right. On January 2, 1954, Sir James Robertson and Mr George Woodcock, of the British T.U.C., arrived in Georgetown where they were joined by Sir Donald Jackson, a Guyanese who was then Chief Justice of the Windward and Leeward Islands. Their brief: the Suspension of the Constitution.

The P.P.P. decided to boycott the Commission. The *Fortnightly* (May 1954) said Sir James Robertson

Anti-Party Activities

'. . . rather took the wind out of the P.P.P. sails at his initial press conference, when he announced his Commission would inquire fully into the circumstances leading to the suspension of the Constitution (which the P.P.P. had said he would not do) and . . . (said) . . . the Commission was free to recommend the re-institution of the (Waddington) Constitution.'

The *Fortnightly* thought the P.P.P. 'had lost a good opportunity to sabotage the proceedings'. But the Robertson Commission in their report rather tartly commented, 'The Party leaders by coming forward would have rendered themselves liable to public questioning on matters of some difficulty'.

The Commission worked on until early March and when its report was tabled in the House of Commons, its main suggestions were that there should be 'a period of marking time'. The London *Times Weekly Review* commented,

'the length of the period will depend upon the extent to which the people of British Guiana, including the leaders of the P.P.P., can be brought to realize that the future and deliberately disruptive policies for which the P.P.P. at present stands are no basis for the future constitutional progress of their country.'

The one certain thing the Commission had been able to say was that the majority of the voters would still go on backing the P.P.P. at any time in the future that they were given a chance.

Some idea of P.P.P. popularity can be seen from the same article in the *Fortnightly*, the correspondent reported, 'A meeting of the party executive in a private house in Georgetown last January attracted to the street outside a crowd that quickly grew to 4,000 or 5,000 and had to be dispersed by the police'.

However right the Commission may have been over the need for a period of marking time, it was exactly the opposite to what the Governor had told the new, entirely nominated, government that he had brought into existence on January

5th that year. Then he had said that he did not want to think that the budget he had put forward was a 'marking time budget' nor indeed that they were a 'marking time government.'

Nor historically was it. It changed the face of Guyana. The sugar workers, who until then had been living in the insanitary ranges, began to get grants to build houses, roads were improved, drainage and irrigation extended, more opportunities to rent or buy land was offered to the agricultural worker, and capital development took place. And in London, the Directors of Bookers made Sir (then Mr) Jock Campbell the Chairman of the group – who as a Socialist set about giving Bookers a new look and opening the road of promotion to Guyanese.

But the people of Guyana recognized that this had only happened because the P.P.P. had fought the British Government and the sugar companies, and their gratitude went to Jagan and Burnham.

With Jagan and Burnham back the party once again began to feel the internal strains. In March, it started a Civil Disobedience campaign and in April Cheddi Jagan was sent to prison for six months hard labour.

Others had been arrested before and the progressive wing of the P.P.P. then found itself in difficulties. Burnham and his followers did not believe in being sent to jail at that time, especially as they saw that by remaining out they could counteract the effects of the 1953 party elections that had left them in the minority.

The Party split came in February of the next year, 1955, and subsequently the P.P.P. (Jaganite) as it was then called issued a 25 page pamphlet called *The Great Betrayal*. In it they blamed the machinations of the British (in that the Robertson Commission had recommended that the P.P.P. ought to get rid of the extremists) and of Mr R. B. O. Hart who was the editor of the *Clarion*. As has been seen the split goes back to the 1947 offer of party leadership to Burnham but as the quotation in *The Great Betrayal* has frequently been repeated and has developed a certain myth-like quality, it is only fair to quote it again in full. *The Great Betrayal*

Anti-Party Activities

reports Mr Hart as saying,

'On July 25, 1954 I sold Burnham an idea which he is now putting into practice. I quote the *Clarion* of that date:

' "You owe a duty to the people of this country who have followed you blindly. So far you have been lucky. You have done nothing to merit their blind support and idolatry. How can you as a young man of any character and decency lead them astray again? You and Dr J. P. Lachhmansingh would make a very effective team, if you stood hand in hand you would be able to keep the Party together while kicking the extremists out. Lachhmansingh is no spring chicken himself, but is one of the few men in your Party of whom I would say, he is not a Communist".'

But Mr Hart is being given credit for something that is hardly his due. His suggestion that Burnham, who could bring in the Negro vote, should join with Lachhmansingh and Jai Naraine Singh, whom it was thought would attract the Indian voter, was nothing less than obvious. Neither Hart nor the Robertson Commission sowed the seeds of discontent. It was the Jagans who had done this when Dr Jagan became the leader of the party over Burnham. From that moment Burnham was certain to either try to regain his leadership, or to form his own party.

In December 1954, Burnham found himself chairing an Executive Committee meeting where he had, by using his casting vote as Chairman, a majority. A motion was passed that as no Congress had been held since 1953 one should be held as soon as possible and a date in January was agreed upon. On the date suggested Janet Jagan and other Jaganites would still be in prison and it was subsequently agreed that the Congress would be on February 12th and 13th.

The Jaganites had a number of their supporters in prison, others were 'restricted' and were not allowed to attend any political meeting. Throughout January and February, the Burnhamites remained in control of the Executive Committee, but the Jaganites had a slight majority in the General

Council, which would have had the power to over-rule the decisions to hold a Congress. The Jaganites called a General Council, but though they had a majority, they did not have sufficient for a quorum. When the Burnhamites stayed away, there was nothing else to do but to accept that the Congress would be held.

There is little to be gained by recounting the proposals and counter-proposals and the alleged statements by the two groups. On February 12th the Jaganites boycotted the meeting, but they were forced to attend the second meeting, the next day, which was to be held at the Metropole Cinema opposite P.P.P. headquarters. Had they not attended, elections would have been held and they would have lost control of the whole party machinery.

After considerable negotiations, Burnham agreed to a fixed agenda and, also, that there would not be 'Members' Motions' or 'Any Other Business'. The Jaganites believed that they had successfully blocked any attempt to hold elections for party office. It is interesting that of the eight points on the agenda, 'The Party and Race' was one. This showed that it had already become a problem and that both Jaganites and Burnhamites were willing, or possibly wanted, to discuss it on a purely theoretical plane.

The meeting had only just opened when Clinton Wong jumped to his feet and moved to suspend 'Standing Rules and Orders'. The Chairman (Burnham) punctiliously said that he was not prepared to allow this unless he knew what it was about. Wong said he wanted to move a motion of 'No Confidence' against the present Executive Committee.

One must admire the fine legal distinction with which the Chairman's mind had looked ahead at the time he agreed to there being neither 'Members' Motions' nor 'Any Other Business' – a vote of 'no confidence' is something different.

The rest of the story cannot be better told than in the words of *The Great Betrayal*:

'The Chairman then conferred with the thirteen available members present on the platform. Several of these thirteen members objected to the suspension of the "Standing Rules

Anti-Party Activities

and Orders" as being in violation of the decision of an exclusive agenda. The Chairman, however, ruled that he would permit the motion for the Suspension of the "Standing Rules and Orders". At that moment, Dr Jagan rose on a point of order to challenge the ruling of the Chairman which violated the decision of the Executive Committee. The Chairman persisted in his ruling to allow the suspension of the "Standing Rules and Orders". The General Secretary who was sitting next to the Chairman on the platform said this to him just before the "walk out" – "The Unity of the Party is in your hands now. If you go ahead as you are doing, the Party will be split. I place the full responsibility in your hands". This the Chairman ignored and it was at this stage that Comrades C. Jagan, Janet Jagan, Martin Carter, Rory Westmaas, George Robertson, Fred Bowman and Lionel Jeffrey left the Conference. They were followed by about 200 floor members.'

The party was then split into P.P.P. (Jaganites) and P.P.P. (Burnhamites). They were beginning to pay the price for the broken promise over the leadership.

Over a year later, when new elections that would finally decide to whom the P.P.P. belonged were in the offing, Burnham was in Jamaica and was asked why the split had taken place and what its effect would be. The *Daily Gleaner* quoted him as saying:

'The People's Progressive Party is now two parties which once was one. *Our differences are ideological and tactical.*

'I for one have no power over a man who says he is a Communist and who thinks that every gyration of Stalin when he was in office was inspired by genius. That is his business! I have no power over a man who because Stalin abuses Tito thinks in British Guiana he should also abuse Tito.

'What I say is although a man is free to follow any ideology he wants, he must not jeopardise a national movement. It is my conviction that the People's Progressive Party was not a Communist party. It was *not* seeking to institute a Communist dictatorship: what I say is that the British Government used certain isolated incidents, and certain people's declarations that they were Communists as an excuse to the world to isolate British Guiana when her Constitution was suspended.

'A national movement cannot afford to be sectarian, and you cannot behave in such a way as to give the impression that your party is a Communist party; for the national movement as the one in our area, it is nothing short of suicide under the peculiar geographical conditions to be shouting to the World that you are a Communist.'

At about the same time Frank Hill, also writing in the *Daily Gleaner* summed up his, a West Indian view, of Jagan and Burnham's character.

Jagan, he said, was essentially an Indian whose Marxist thinking was unaffected by an inner cultural conflict, but Burnham:

'Burnham is a West Indian Negro, torn several ways by conflicting influences. A European education grounds him in ways of political thinking that appear to offer a solution to his country's problems. So Marxism becomes the chosen instrument. But even with the choice come many anxious doubts which exploded in his mind after October 1953.

'Did I make these mistakes because I'm incapable of responsibility? Are we West Indian Negroes unfit to be trusted with power because we're inferior, as they say in South Africa? Can I prove we're equal to White men?

'So Burnham came to have a second look at the chosen instrument; searched vainly along it for answers to the questions that only a West Indian can be urged to ask. For Africa, within West Indian thinking, provides no independent influential political fount of racial pride as yet; and the language, religion and social customs of the region are borrowed articles with the use of which we are only now coming to familiarize ourselves consciously.'

What would the next elections show? But before that there had to be a regrouping of the forces.

Chapter 16

THE NEW GAME

1955 HAD begun with the P.P.P. split and it was to go out with some Christmas excitement. On December 25th, three newspapers announced that a game was on sale in Hungary (evidently similar to *Diplomacy*) in which Georgetown was shown 'ringed in red'. Get Georgetown, implied the rules of the game, and you are a fair way to being President of the United Soviet States of America.

All three papers editorialized on the seriousness of the Communist threat.

Others too were worried, including the new Governor, Sir Patrick Renison, who had arrived at the end of October, charged with designing a new constitution and a new political way of life for the colony.

In January 1956 the Jamaica *Daily Gleaner* said: 'Apathy threatens to destroy British Guiana and finish the job deliberate sabotage nearly did two years ago' and quoting from *New Commonwealth*, 'since the People's Progressive Party leaders were thrown out of office and some went to jail, no new champion of the people has arisen'.

In April Governor Renison proposed a constitution with a Legislative Council of twelve elected members, exactly equalled by four ex-officio and eight nominated. Under this Constitution he said there would probably be elections in 1957.

People began to think wistfully and optimistically of their chances of winning something and there was considerable lobbying at the top levels, with people forming new parties, or threatening to, in the hope of strengthening their bargaining positions.

Nobody, however, except the P.P.P. (Jaganites), was prepared to go out into the countryside and win votes. The P.P.P. (Burnhamites) and United Democratic Party (U.D.P.) did not mind going out on a Saturday or Sunday afternoon to hold a meeting. But they had no organization and would have been shocked had anyone suggested that they stayed out overnight and built up personal contacts and got to know the people's problems.

They preferred optimism to work. John Carter, Leader of the U.D.P., when asked by a reporter about the Renison Constitution was critical of it and said, 'the British Government had failed to realize that several persons had changed their attitude since 1953 and the voters who supported the People's Progressive Party would not vote that way again'! So much for what the U.D.P. knew!

In October the Colonial Secretary and the Governor announced minor changes in the Renison Constitution – two more elected members, plus three more nominated, less one ex-officio – but the equation remained the same: elected members had to be equalled by ex-officio plus nominated, so that there could be no question of any elected party forming a majority.

When the news reached Georgetown of the new definitive form, an all-party conference was held that unanimously rejected it. All parties called for a restoration of the Waddington Constitution, which even the P.P.P. would, by then, have welcomed with open arms. The parties continued to complain for the next twelve months, but the Colonial Office remained adamant and the elections were fought under the revised Renison Constitution.

But if the other parties were relying on optimism, the P.P.P. (Jaganites) had been going through a period of intense self-criticism and Cheddi Jagan produced with his Executive Committee an analysis of their position.

This formed the basis of his speech to the Annual Congress in 1956. It has always been P.P.P. policy for the Leader and Executive Members' speeches to be given behind closed doors

The New Game

with all members of the public excluded. However, in 1956 Cheddi Jagan was restricted to Georgetown, and other members were also restricted in the countryside. This was the one occasion when copies of the Leader's Congress Speech were made and sent to branch members. The Georgetown *Daily Chronicle*, not normally the most reliable source for P.P.P. news, was able to buy a copy of the speech off a P.P.P. member for $50 (£10). The P.P.P. have never denied it, and there is no reason to believe that the text of what has come to be called 'Dr Jagan's Secret Address of 1956' has been tampered with at all.

The speech does drop the veil for a moment and give a glimpse of top level P.P.P. thinking among the Jaganites. Having begun with a quick view of the international scene, Bandung, defeat of Imperialist France in Indo-China, the hydrogen bomb exploded in the Soviet Union, and so had been able to assure his listeners that their strength outside was growing. he turned to internal affairs and especially the U.D.P.

It was the U.D.P., he said, that the British Government had hoped, by bringing their members into the Interim Government, would be able to win the political confidence of the people. However, the U.D.P. failed to win over the countryside and the British Government had turned to Lionel Luckhoo in the hope that he could form an Indian party under the title National Labour Front (N.L.F.).

The split in the P.P.P. he explained in this way:

'The basis of the split was a deal with the imperialists. The imperialists on their part would grant elections, the Burnhamites on their part would guarantee to form a Government either by taking over the leadership of the Party and changing its policies, or by splitting from the "Communist" faction with a decisive strength and following. This strength was to be based on 11 constituencies, 5 in Georgetown behind Burnham and 6 in the Demerara suger estate areas behind Lachhmansingh.'

Jagan remarks that Lachhmansingh found himself unable

to swing over the Indian estate workers and Burnham had been forced to appeal to African racialism, to anti-Communism and demagogy.

'To understand the P.P.P. split is to understand the forces supporting and operating behind Burnham. Burnham's background is entirely middle-class. His father was a schoolmaster. This has resulted in his close association with professionals, school teachers, civil servants, other sections of the middle-class and away from the soil, from direct contact with the toiling masses.'

Before he asks what the P.P.P. should do, Jagan asks first,

'What is the P.P.P.? The P.P.P. is a national party, a broad alliance of various democratic sections – working class, peasantry, middle-class, native businessmen and capitalists – opposed to imperialism. As such, communists, social-democrats, native capitalists, civil servants, professional men can all play their part in, and belong to, such a party.
'Our Party is unique in the history of national movements in that from the very inception it was under left-wing Marxist-inspired leadership uncompromisingly championing the cause of the working class. The right-wing, representing the middle and professional class and native capitalists, was in the distinct minority.'

One important thing, however, for the Party at the present time was to keep the native capitalist on their side – in fact everybody they could, regardless of class or political interests. Jagan looks back at what they had had in 1953 when they had come to power:

'. . . supporting our party were:–
(1) the overwhelming mass of workers and farmers of all races.
(2) Section of the middle-class civil servants, professionals, teachers, etc.
(3) Indian sections of native commercial and industrial

The New Game

capitalist, as distinct from Indian landlords.
(4) Sections of African native capitalists.

Portuguese native capitalists and landlords of Indian and other races together with a few other Indian and African merchants were generally opposed to us.'

They had achieved this by their 'successful manoeuvre in breaking Burnham and Chase' away from those who were basically Negro orientated. Ashton Chase was in England at that time and that people assumed he would join Burnham – hence his name being associated with Burnham. Chase returned just a few days before the elections and, after attending one of Burnham's meetings, suddenly decided that he would stay with the Jagans.

It is unfortunate that the details of how they 'manoeuvred' Burnham and Chase is lost, as at that point about 180 words are missing from the original. When it starts again, Jagan is referring to Comrade Stalin who in 1925 defined three categories of colonies. Which Jagan asked is B.G.? And came to the conclusion that it was at an intermediate stage between the first with no proletariat and no industry and the second, as was the China and Egypt of those days, with some proletariat and some industry.

Having determined the historical position, Cheddi Jagan then laid down the policy that should be followed:

Of 1953,
'We definitely under-rated the importance of an alliance between the working class and the revolutionary bourgeoisie against imperialism, it is our task, therefore, to lay the basis for forging such an alliance. As a start our party has issued a call to all political organizations to join us in a joint demand for restoration of constitutional life and end of all emergency restrictions. It is not too much to reveal that talks are now going on between the Burnham faction, the U.D.P. and ourselves on this question.

'Some comrades, however, feel that the three "parties" must proceed immediately to the formation of a united national front which will include a programme and electoral plans (division of seats, etc). It should be noted that a national front can be, or become, an electoral front, but does not necessarily mean an electoral front.

'We are primarily interested in struggle – Messrs Burnham and John Carter are primarily interested in "Office". If they are not really interested in struggle, in taking firm and resolute action in support of our demands, then there is no advantage in such a national front. In such a situation, we have everything to lose and nothing to gain. We will have to make concessions to them with regard to electoral seats. We will have to share our platform with them at joint meetings and expose our "territory" to their reactionary ideas. There will be the danger of right deviationism towards all unity and no struggle.

'With a united front common programme and the use by them of left phraseology and demagogy, the masses will experience great difficulty in comprehending the differences between us.

'Let me now illustrate this danger. All the time Burnham was with us, we had to control his right deviationist tendencies, at the same time not expose him for fear of disrupting our party. In 1952, after my motion in the Legislative Council asking Government to lift the ban on the entry of Billy Strachan and Ferdinand Smith, the Burnham faction seriously objected and passed a motion in the Executive of our party, demanding that all motions I introduce in the Legislative Council must have the prior approval of the Executive Committee of the Party.

'Procedurally, they were correct; although the practice was established because I was a member of the Legislative Council before the formation of the Party. But what must be noted was not so much their objection to procedure, but their objection to the content of the resolution.

'In other words, the Burnham clique were prepared to deviate to the right, to sacrifice our proletarian working class, internationalist outlook for narrow nationalism.'

In the end Dr Jagan suggested that they should strike a

The New Game

middle course 'Unity and Struggle', in other words of 'enlarging and consolidating the left-wing group, of urging the middle group to progress and change, and of isolating the right-wing group . . ', which, he pointed out, was a paraphrase of Mao Tse Tung's teaching.

There was one great issue at the time. Whether the West Indies should Federate or not. It was difficult, in a world that needs large units to industrialize efficiently, for Jagan to argue against it. Yet every Indian knew that it might bring an influx of Negroes that could counter-act their increasing population. The Negro themselves were not entirely happy about Federation as they feared any political gains might be offset by increasing unemployment or under-employment.

Having pointed out these facts, directly or by implication, Dr Jagan then gave the meeting the lead, 'The Indians feeling as they do a sense of national oppression are almost 100% opposed to Federation'. He then explained that by discussing joining the Federation one might be able to get an agreement to Dominion Status. His recommendation was that the Party should support participation in a West Indian Federation on a basis of Dominion status, but that the final decision should only be determined by a Referendum – that is, having gained Dominion Status, at least in principle, the Indian could then turn down Federation if he wanted to.

Cheddi Jagan's speech was to explain much that came later, as for instance the remark in 1957 Manifesto, 'The P.P.P. welcomes the new West Indian Federation.'

So by the time the elections came, the P.P.P. (Jaganites) had reorganized and stood as the defenders of the people whose leaders had gone to jail for them. More than anything else, race was in politics and the murmur went round, 'Aphan Jhat', 'Vote Race', which meant vote P.P.P. (Jaganite).

The P.P.P. had proved it could use the dialectic when in opposition, but unfortunately it had not been back long in power before the analysis went out of the window. Personalities distorted the party machinery, and Dr Jagan, who had so roundly condemned leftist-deviationism, was making speeches that were bound to ensure all struggle and no unity at all.

Chapter 17

NEW BEHAVIOUR

As everyone expected, when the election results were announced the Jaganite P.P.P. came romping home with nine seats out of fourteen. The P.P.P. (Burnhamites) won only the three Georgetown seats. The N.L.F. contested every seat and won only one which was the North-west because its candidate was Mr Stephen Campbell, who always wins there regardless of party. The U.D.P. only contested eight seats but their fate was identical: while there is a New Amsterdam constituency and a Mr W. O. Kendall, he will be elected. He is known as 'the favourite son' but by reputation he has seen himself as something older than this.

So ended, *de facto* at least, the N.L.F. and the U.D.P. The 1953 elections had shown that politics were for professional parties and if the N.L.F. and U.D.P. had not learnt the lesson, the independents had, there were only six candidates (as compared to seventy-nine in 1953) and a one man party (one candidate and 199 votes) and they won no seats at all.

The parties were still not well organized – or rather the one large party, the P.P.P. was not, as only 40% of the electorate voted. This time the P.P.P. won only 47% of the votes cast instead of 51%. It was not such a great come back as all that.

No party had been willing to join with the P.P.P. so there had been no question of an 'electoral front', but Dr Jagan in an interview with the *Daily Gleaner* said he intended to run a 'clean stable government' (the Interim Government had a reputation that was far from irreproachable over money matters) and 'foreign capital will have the full protection it enjoys under existing laws. I do *not* plan any drastic changes.

New Behaviour

I want to keep things running smoothly'. The watchwords were to be Mao Tse Tung's 'Unity and Struggle', and each was to apply both to Guyanese parties and to the British Government.

On August 20, 1957 in what can only be called a noble remark Burnham conceded the name P.P.P. 'Dr Jagan is entitled to it. He won'. Six weeks later Burnham announced his party's name was to be the Peoples' National Congress (P.N.C.) and its paper, *New Nation*. Asked whether he was considering rejoining the P.P.P., Burnham replied sharply, 'I will not be made a tool twice.'

With nine out of fourteen seats, Dr Jagan was in a position of strength. In his 1956 'Secret Address', he had told his audience that the Indian Congress Party had successfully fought against the 1935 elections by being overwhelmingly voted into power, forming a ministry and then promptly resigning – offering to repeat the performance *ad nauseam* until the British government gave them more freedom. It seems probable that Dr Jagan reminded the Governor of this when he went to discuss the formation of a Government.

As in 1953, there was to be a long period before any official announcement was made, but this time it was not because there was division in the P.P.P. It was Dr Jagan holding out for the right to decide whom some of the nominated members should be and so to give himself a majority.

He first saw the Governor on Saturday August 17th. Eleven days later Renison gave in. His only strength now lay in his Reserve Powers. He agreed that the P.P.P. should put forward the names of three of the members, so giving themselves, nine elected plus three of their own nominated members against eleven elected and nominated of the opposition – a majority of one. But more important, in the Executive Council they won for themselves five against three official members.

Cheddi Jagan took Trade and Industry and Janet Jagan, Labour, Health and Housing. She had always been regarded with considerable respect as a party organizer and worker, even by those who disliked her, but with this term of office, she won for herself the general recognition as the one P.P.P. Minister who was efficient and effective. A scheme that she started of Village Health Centres is a lasting memorial to her integrity and energy and must have more greatly improved the lives of the people than any other direct action the P.P.P. took.

Cheddi Jagan had got off to a flying start. John Carter told a reporter he was a changed man and 'has made a wonderful start. . . . Many people who were opposed to Jagan now say, thank God Jagan won.'

Generally press comment was favourable saying that Jagan obviously had the popular support of the country; this was his second chance and everyone wished him well. *The Times British Colonies Review* ended an editorial by saying, 'On balance the great advantage is that the log jam in British Guiana has been shifted. But nobody should under-estimate the difficulties of guiding the logs downstream to harbour'.

However by the end of October, a small cloud did appear on the horizon. Mr Neville Annibourne announced a two day youth conference for November 9th to 10th 'to unite the youth of all races between the ages of 16 and 35'.

The *Guiana Graphic* in its editorial suggested that the Governor and public should 'keep a sharp eye on what comes along out of the forthcoming P.P.P. Youth Rally'. But the first conference of the Progressive Youth Organization (P.Y.O.) came and went and Renison felt he could end the Emergency Order that had been in existence since October 8, 1953.

If the 'non-communists' saw this as a threat, the P.P.P. by the end of November was beginning to forget is maxim of Unity and Struggle and took the first step to alienate the Civil Service. The Civil Service was both largely Negro and was certainly privileged and it was seen by the P.P.P., at least on the second count, as an enemy. In 1956 Dr Jagan had said, 'Time and circumstance must be taken into account. This is how the history of the C.P.S.U. put it: "The Marxist-Leninist Theory must not be regarded as a collection of dogmas, as a catechism, as a symbol of faith, and the Marxists themselves as pedants and dogmatists".' By 1957, he saw things differently. He forgot that for the P.P.P. to govern it had to have the Civil Service, if not on its side, at least neutralized. Instead the

New Behaviour

P.P.P. decided to put on a show of strength by announcing that as most of the Service was now composed of Guyanese it would stop the payment of fares to the U.K. for Civil Service families on long leave. Perfectly logical, but this with other measures was to drive the professional grades in the Civil Service Association (C.S.A.) to seek affiliation with the T.U.C. and on two occasions to leave the government with hardly any administration at most critical times.

In December, Burnham, not to be outdone by the P.Y.O., started the National Young People's Movement. The name was changed during the conference to El Dorado Youth Alliance: a name that was to reflect closely its connexion with fantasy.

In 1958, the P.P.P. called its sixth Congress and demanded independence by 1960. There was a merger expected between the P.N.C. and the virtually defunct U.D.P. (as represented by Mr Kendall). The P.N.C. supported the P.P.P. in the Legislative Council in a joint appeal for self-government, but the P.N.C. also wanted Federation and the P.P.P. did not, so the support was not very significant.

Then in June 1958, the Governor and Dr Jagan with Edward Beharry, Minister for National Resources, set off to London to try to get some more money for the colony.

It was at this time that Jagan forgot both dialectics and his own good advice. He left saying that his government might resign if not given forty million pounds. Or else, and here came the threat, 'he will look elsewhere'. He was also going to ask for constitutional changes.

Dr Jagan was forgetting 'time and circumstances'. People were still on his side. The London *Times* said in an editorial that 'After a year's good conduct . . .' he would have a right to expect something better than he had at present. The Jamaica *Gleaner*, having got the tone of Dr Jagan's remarks, thought there was little hope of his getting all he wanted or so quickly, anyway it estimated Guyana did not have the technical personnel and detailed projects to absorb more than eight million pounds annually, so what was all this fuss about forty million?

The *Gleaner's* London correspondent thought that Jagan's

Trouble in Guyana

threats to seek aid 'elsewhere' or to resign and 'let the Colonial Office try to sort out the mess' were ill-timed, especially as in 'responsible circles' he was still considered a political risk.

Dr Jagan had completely forgotten his own good advice. While in London he addressed a meeting of 300 West Indian students. He lashed out at Britain and praised, Nehru, Nasser and Nkrumah, but the audience was not entirely friendly, when he asked rhetorically, 'Where do we go from here?' He got the reply 'Home'. And, 'If we don't get money here, where are we going to get it?', the ironic reply came back, 'Go *East*, young man'.

He told the press, 'If Britain cannot run British Guiana we might as well let the United Nations run it'. But he got five and a half million pounds for 1958 and 1959 and flew off to Canada with the delegation looking for aid from there.

He didn't get much more than promises, but when he arrived back he said that he hoped all the parties would join and they could all go to London and 'demand' help. He told the people that the Governor, who had been with him, 'had done his best' and then he and Janet Jagan and Mr and Mrs Beharry all got into a truck carrying slogans 'We oppose Colonialism' and 'Freedom for British Guiana Now' and they drove into Georgetown from the airport.

In their absence things had gone wrong for Mr Beharry. There was talk of match concessions being drawn up in a strange way. Only a week after their return Beharry addressed a meeting at Enmore and said 'I disagree that an economic crisis faces British Guiana today' and went on to say that all that was needed was more publicity and investors would come pouring in.

The *History of the P.P.P.* under the heading 'Internal Trouble' says it another way:

'There is no doubt that the Party had internal troubles during the four year term of office and the case of Edward Beharry is one that all recall. There are many who seem to forget that he was removed from office at the request of the Majority Party . . . and one would imagine from his outbursts in the Legislative Council that he threw over the P.P.P.

New Behaviour

The decision of the P.P.P. to remove Beharry from office is a concrete example of the high standards which the Party maintained. . . .'

Jagan did call for an all-party coalition to fight the British, but the U.D.P. refused to consider it, the P.N.C. refused but said they 'would welcome a general election' and the non-existent N.L.F. agreed on the necessity for all-party unity.

That ended the suggestion and in November all the parties girded their loins when Renison appointed a Constitutional Commission under Sir Donald Jackson as Chairman (no vote) three *ex-officio* members (no vote) and all the Legislative Council. Quite obviously how the Constitution was decided affected all parties; seven years later it has still not been decided.

1959 was very much a repetition of 1958. The U.D.P. merged with the P.N.C., adding one vote, but Jai Naraine Singh left, taking away one vote, and formed his Guyana Independence Movement (G.I.M.) which demanded independence immediately. This remained its only platform and it would be hardly unfair to say that G.I.M.'s sole adherent today is – Jai Naraine Singh.

In June Jagan once again set off for Britain in search of aid and for a seven week, almost annual, trip. In August he was in Bonn looking for money. On his way back at Port of Spain he told journalists that Britain's £23 million loan guarantees were not enough and said that he thought of taking one from the 'Russian market strictly on a commercial basis, and especially in view of the fact that Russia's rate of interest was much lower than other countries'.

Back in Guyana, he said there was 'every indication' that he could get a substantial loan and spoke of getting a mandate by referendum 'or some such thing' as otherwise 'we might be faced with a suspension of the constitution'.

If one wishes to judge how far he had moved away from the discipline of the dialectic there is a further reported interview when he said, 'I was told the other day that if all the monies now spent for armaments and defence were diverted to development *our share* would be about $US60 million per year.'

But if things seemed to be going on more or less the same there were also problems. The P.N.C. had worked out that its only hope lay in Proportional Representation and started to demand a new electoral system. And in December, the failure of the government to implement an independent report on the salaries and working conditions of the Civil Service had brought about a fifteen day strike by the lower echelons of the Service – already the upper echelons had joined the T.U.C. – and were prepared to strike if necessary. Dr Jagan only gave in after a half-hour talk with the Acting Governor.

No agreed Constitution had been worked out by March 1960 when delegates from different parties went to London to discuss the future of the colony. Essentially, the P.P.P. could not get P.N.C. support as they did not want Federation and the P.N.C. did. However, the Conference did set up a new and advanced form of Legislature with two Houses, a wholly elected Legislative Assembly and a nominated Senate. The next elections would be held the following year, 1961.

While in London, Dr Jagan wrote to the *Daily Worker* congratulating it on its thirtieth anniversary with the ambiguous remark, 'I know from experience, in my own country, that freedom of the Press means control by the reactionary forces.'

As 1960 went on, the strains within the party and the drudgery of everyday government that is disbarred from organizing strikes told its tale. Attempts to win Burnham back had failed and instead such remarks as 'We haven't got battleships or guns, but we have some friends who have rockets and money' made by Dr Jagan hit world headlines. Except for Janet Jagan's health schemes, there was little else except when a member of the Special Branch tried to suborn a secretary in Freedom House (P.P.P. H.Q.) and she informed the party. The detective who kept the rendezvous was met by flash cameras and the government protested strongly against its own police force spying on its own party.

There had been peace and stability but now there were new elections to prepare for.

Chapter 18

SHIFTING ALLIANCES

UNTIL 1960, the story of Guyanese politics has really been of one Party, split from 1955 into two branches, the Indian and the Negro. The Indian under the Jagans considering itself an embryonic Communist Party, the African under Burnham as being nearer the Labour Party. The many attempts to form other parties had all been based on either race, or on similar platforms to the P.P.P., and they had all failed.

In November 1960 a Portuguese pawnbroker, soft-drinks and rum manufacturer, started a new political party that, because of his own background, and vehement, but muddled, feelings was to find for the first time the support of different groups of people that had not before felt any party truly represented them.

To understand his party, it is necessary to see something of his own personality. His family believed that if they could look further back than the period when they came over as indentured labourers they would find some royal blood. The pawnbroking shop they opened was therefore named 'The Imperial House'.

Peter d'Aguiar as the son of a Catholic family was sent to Stonyhurst College and from there to Birmingham University where he gained a degree. In one of the accounts given by his party, the U.F. (United Force), he is said to have risen from 'rags to riches', but the period when he was in rags has not to my knowledge been identified.

He began dabbling in national politics in the 1953 elections when he stood as one of the 79 independents. He did not stand in 1957 but early in 1960 he began to look around for a group that he might lead.

For mass support he turned to three groups, the Portuguese minority, the coloured middle class and the Amerindians. Among these three he had advantages that neither the P.P.P. nor the P.N.C. possessed. Since he was Portuguese he could reasonably expect that, as a minority group, they too would be tempted to vote race. To the coloured middle class, which were largely urban in either the Civil Service or in business, he could offer free enterprise, and to the ranchers and the Amerindians, who were influenced by the Catholic and other Christian missions, he could offer his religious background, including a spell as a fervent member of M.R.A.

For money and leadership he turned to the rich Indians who had either fallen out with the P.P.P. or been expelled.

In those days, the Indian community were seen as the more stable section of the community. Everyone accepted that they were capitalists at heart, and the belief was that one day they would come to their senses and recognize that their personal interests demanded that they should stop voting for Jagan and Communism.

The Negro on the other hand was seen as the unstable element who was not really interested in the creation of a modern and viable society, but only in power and its immediate enjoyment. It was thought that he would be quite content to see Guyana disintegrate into a voodoo state similar to Haiti. The 'blackman' represented violence and rape and the worst forms of disorder.

From the start, d'Aguiar was faced by an enigma. The fate of the U.D.P., the N.L.F., and numerous other small parties, showed that if he tried to go it alone he would most probably be squeezed out of existence at the first elections. He had therefore to arrange some sort of electoral alliance.

As most of his money came from the Indians who had formerly been in the P.P.P., there was a natural reluctance to go there. The only other possibility was to turn to the P.N.C. and, on the premise that the U.F. represented the balance of power, to demand virtual equality. In this way, they might hope to beat the P.P.P. and maintain sufficient

Shifting Alliances

control over the Negro element to ensure a stable government.

The talks were in progress by the middle of 1960; by September the *Sunday Graphic* reported that Burnham had refused to consider an alliance. But in actual fact he managed to keep the United Force, which in desperation had been formed as a separate party in November 1960, on the hook until July 6th the next year. Then Burnham came out publicly with a statement that the P.N.C. would not accept the offers of a merger made by the U.F. The official mimeographed history of the U.F. says the P.N.C. began 'as an African organization when they split from the Jagans in 1955 and they adamantly refused to consider accepting Indians on their Executive in any reasonable proportion to Africans. Valuable time was wasted while some form of compromise was sought with Burnham'. Valuable time was a euphemism, when Burnham finally turned them down, there were only six weeks to go before the elections. It looked very much as though he had wiped out their chances of winning any seats at all.

The U.F. then had no other choice but to turn to the P.P.P. When one has lived in Georgetown following events and reading the newspapers, one begins to sense when to read the opposite to what is printed. On July 30th, the *Chronicle* (a U.F. paper) came out with a lead story that there was collusion between the P.P.P. and the P.N.C. It said they had both agreed *not* to fight in the strongholds of the other, but were going to put up candidates in marginal constituencies.

There are three things that make one suspect this story. The first is that the P.P.P. has never put up candidates in constituencies that it knew it could not win. They have done this for the very good reason that they believe in concentrating their resources and giving each candidate strong outside support. Secondly, if the story had been true, it would have favoured the U.F. who could then have counted on being given all the dissident votes without these being split with the other party. The last reason is that the P.N.C. were at the time over-weeningly confident that they would win and subsequently put up candidates for all the constituencies.

One may therefore be reasonably confident that the story

in the *Chronicle* gives the date when the P.P.P. and the U.F. entered into *their* electoral agreement. The P.P.P. thought they had nothing to fear from the U.F., but wished to reduce the number of seats the P.N.C. might win. They agreed, what they had anyway already decided on, not to contest four seats in Georgetown and one in Rupununi, a largely Amerindian vote.

A recently printed apologia for the P.P.P. has said that there was no such agreement, but Janet Jagan has wryly confirmed that it was true and they were to regret it later. It has also been confirmed by senior members of the U.F.

The force of the U.F. propaganda was from then turned against the P.N.C. And, while still maintaining some anti-Communist propaganda in the hope of picking up some votes, the *Chronicle* tended to shift the responsibility for the articles away from the U.F. This was reflected in the newspaper which one day ran a story with a dateline in New York on the Jagans being Communists, and in its editorial praised Dr Jagan for following U.F. advice, ending up with the single line, 'A word is enough for a wise man'.

The U.F. history says, 'The United Force fought a consistent anti-Communist campaign but it was hampered by the fact that Jagan had not publicly committed himself to Communism. . . '. It was actually hampered by the hope that after the elections it would be able to form a coalition with the P.P.P. and, going back to that recurrent dream in Guyanese politics, it would then be able to restrain the more 'extreme' P.P.P. members.

Both P.P.P. and P.N.C. were to regret what they had done. When d'Aguiar decided to stand for Georgetown Central, Burnham's old seat, Burnham saw the danger and moved out to Ruimveldt, leaving his Chairman, Mrs Gaskin, to fight the battle and lose by 836 votes.

Burnham had been faced with a difficult choice when d'Aguiar proposed a merger and since one can never know on what terms exactly d'Aguiar would have settled, it is impossible to say whether his mistake was a serious error of judgement. But it was not this decision that in the end lost the P.N.C. the election.

Shifting Alliances

For the election each party had chosen a symbol: the P.P.P. a cup; the U.F. a Sun; and the P.N.C. a broom (a besom). Burnham has always maintained that the besom was chosen to show that though one could break each single individual twig quite easily, when they were all bound together they could not be broken. His followers however took up the slogan: 'A broom to sweep them out and keep them out'.

The elections were held on Monday August 21st. On the Sunday P.N.C. supporters came out into the streets armed with brooms. They began chanting their slogans and sweeping dust into the faces of any Indians and Portuguese they met. They surrounded houses and told the people they had better vote P.N.C. otherwise they would come for their wives and daughters. By the end of the day some 15,000 people were roaming the streets and the news swept along the coastline, 'If the P.N.C. wins no one is going to be safe'. The Negro was confirming the image that everyone had of him. In July, Burnham had called the P.P.P. the 'greatest Communists of the century', but after the Sunday demonstrations, Communist government, inefficiency, and everything else, became insignificant and when the people went to the polls they voted race.

When the results of the elections came in the P.P.P. had 42.6% of the votes and twenty seats, the P.N.C. with 41% of the votes had only eleven seats. The U.F. had won four seats, their majorities in the two Georgetown constituencies being only 836 and twenty-seven; if the P.P.P. had split the vote they would have been down to two seats only.

Burnham held a monster meeting at Bourda Green. One of the reporters was so carried away that he wrote 'it would appear that every person in Georgetown attended, so vast was the gathering'. Burnham spoke for nearly two hours denouncing d'Aguiar, the U.F. and the leaders of the Christian churches as traitors who had caused the P.N.C. to lose the election by their short-sighted policies. It was to take him a long time to realize what the Negro image was in Guyana.

The U.F. had contested thirty-four out of thirty-five of the seats, but they were pleased with the result – and with the P.P.P. The *Chronicle* published a cartoon showing Cheddi

Jagan paddling a girl (labelled 'voters') across the sea of 'Internal Self-Government' to an island of tropical paradise: from the size of the suitcase behind the girl she was going to spend some time with him. It was captioned, 'Congratulations Cheddi'.

The editorial said, 'The election has, in fact, extended British Guiana's political experience, and given it, for the first time, a maturity that will benefit all the peoples of the land. *The imbalance has gone*; there are more and more new views in our political councils'. It ended on the happy note, 'So, as a nation united in an effort to bring prosperity through self-reliance, let us go forward into the promising realms that beckon us and our children.'

The next day banner headlines proclaimed 'Conquering Hero Returns to City', as Cheddi Jagan led in a two-mile procession of motor cars. The Editorial pointed out that the paper had been critical of the government over the past four years '. . . but (we) are cautiously optimistic about its future actions'. And after quoting some very guarded remarks from all the major newspapers of the world, the editorial writer remarked, 'It is significant that the foreign press is more cautious in acclaiming the new Government than the Guyanese themselves' – a mild attack of xenophobia?

The honeymoon went on the next day, the editorial had the now doubly ironic title, 'The Irony of it All'. It announced that they were amused to read the comment by Moscow Radio on the results of the election. Moscow Radio had said, 'The elections have brought complete victory for the forces of the left in British Guiana. . . . Despite blackmailings and provocations against the party of Dr Jagan, the people have achieved an overwhelming victory over the forces of reaction and colonialism.'

The editorial writer says there was no 'blackmail' used against the P.P.P. and no provocations and then blandly states '. . . the two parties that fought the P.P.P. were *socialist and democratic* and both abhorred colonialism'.

The U.F. have always had a conveniently short memory.

Improbable as it was to seem later, d'Aguiar did manage to build up a relationship with the P.P.P. Soon after the elec-

Shifting Alliances

tions Dr Jagan appointed Mr Jack Kelshall as his Private Secretary and Public Relations Officer. Jack Kelshall was a Trinidadian lawyer with a very good practice, well-off, and a Marxist. He had known the Jagans for many years and in coming to Georgetown he made very considerable personal sacrifices. He was later to become one of the chief U.F. targets, but at that time it was different.

Kelshall called on d'Aguiar and according to the U.F. history, told him that he and Dr Jagan were leaving for the United States in an attempt to muster support for the P.P.P. d'Aguiar then asked what he hoped to achieve. Kelshall is reported to have said, 'To put it bluntly, it's blackmail'.

The rest of the conversation, including d'Aguiar's reply, is left unrecorded by the U.F. historian and one has to turn to its paper the *Chronicle* to find any reaction. On the day following the departure of Dr Jagan it published a cartoon showing Cheddi Jagan standing in front of a house marked 'USA'. The two steps up to the front door have 'Welcome' written on them. Jagan is carrying a large bouquet marked 'Confidence' and he is saying, 'I hope that Uncle Sam will approve', the caption reads, 'The $100 million dollar courtship'. Blackmail is not mentioned.

Even before Jagan got back the honeymoon was wearing thin – it was 'Premier Cheddi Jagan' who left to a 'rousing send-off', but it was 'the P.P.P. Boss', who according to the *Chronicle* headlines, returned.

There were two reasons for this. The first, possibly the more important, Cheddi Jagan made a hash of his American visit. When he arrived in the States, there was quite a strong feeling in the State Department that if he were given Aid he could at least be kept away from the wildest excesses and might even be tamed. But when Jagan went on television with a very wide, if not nation-wide, link-up he was naturally asked for the thousandth time whether he was a Communist. Jagan has never been able to resist falling for this question. His best of a collection of bad answers, comes when he is tired or a little nervous, then he merely says 'My own personal views are my own business, but my party is *not* Communist'. But at other times, he takes the centre of the stage with a slightly hurt look as though once again he were going to be persecuted. He then starts, 'Well, it depends on what you mean by Communism', or 'I am a Marxist-Leninist. . . '. This goes on until anyone who is listening is convinced that he is a raving Communist that has not the courage to say so. The effect on the American audience can well be imagined. They deluged the T.V. station, and the State Department, with such a swirl of letters that the charm of Dr Jagan's courtship with the United States died before it began.

The second was the U.F. discovered that, although the P.P.P. had been willing to engage in a little electoral support in the battle against the P.N.C., they were certainly not in the slightest interested on U.F. views or opinions.

This became apparent when the U.F. tried to discuss the government's taking control of the denominational schools, a number of them Catholic; these were all heavily subsidised by the tax-payer. Nobody in the P.P.P. cared at all about what d'Aguiar or the U.F. or anyone thought of their actions.

With the failure to obtain an American loan and to influence P.P.P. policy, the grand design of taming the P.P.P. had to be given up. It was obvious that however much bad feeling there might be between the P.N.C. and the U.F., it was only in that direction that his small party could hope to find a way to survive. In the meantime, the U.F. had begun its anti-Communist campaign in all seriousness.

A few months later a large part of the commercial centre was burnt to the ground in the struggle between the P.P.P. and the U.F. But after questioning d'Aguiar and a U.F. Senator, the Inquiry Commission decided, 'The list of their grievances against the P.P.P. is little more that a narrative of personal frustration.'

Chapter 19

REFUGE IN VIOLENCE

BURNHAM had been extremely bitter about the success of the U.F. Until then, Guyana had been divided between the P.P.P. and the P.N.C., both claiming to be Socialist and both firmly set, for all they might say on racial lines. The intrusion of the U.F. brought in complications that neither of them had thought of. The P.P.P. were to continue to under-estimate the U.F. until February of the next year, 1962, but the P.N.C. were forced to take a more realistic view once they had lost two seats in their stronghold, Georgetown.

As they looked back on the election they began to wonder whether they had allowed their last chance to pass by them. If the P.P.P. had the patience and skill to sit out the next four years, they were virtually certain, with the rapidly increasing Indian population, to win that election and every election afterwards. The Jagans were building up a reputation for invulnerability: they could take any number of splits, any number of defections, and still go on to win elections.

As always following any defeat, there was much self-criticism in the P.N.C. and, from immoderate self-confidence, they now swung to angry pessimism.

But they still had some good cards. With the P.P.P. refusal to admit the U.F. to its councils they at least had one party that might co-operate with them and together they represented 57% of the voters. Included in this were the Guyanese business community, the urban population and any moderate or right-wing people who did not identify themselves, before everything else, with the Indian vote. Added to this, and their strongest single card, was the fear and dissatisfaction felt by the trade unions.

Although logic demanded that they should form an alliance with the U.F., it was the P.P.P. that brought it about. The spark was the increasing bitterness felt by d'Aguiar over the P.P.P. betrayal, the train to the gunpowder barrel was the P.P.P. treatment of the Civil Servants.

It has already been mentioned that the P.P.P. saw the existing Civil Service as its natural enemy and believed that, as with the trade unions, it must dominate it. The P.P.P. not only openly showed its feelings by setting up its own channels, through P.P.P. supporters, in the Service, and so by-passing those whom it felt were against it, but it also allowed very real grievances to fester.

The cost of living had been rising steadily in Guyana, but while employees in business and the workers had been receiving increased wages, the Civil Service had to look back as far as 1954 to the last Commission, the Hands-Jakeway, that had made any acceptable recommendations on which the government had been prepared to act. Since then, the cost of living had increased by at least 10%. In 1957 the P.P.P. had formed the Gorsuch Commission, but the Civil Service Association representing the higher grades and the Federation of the Unions of Government Employees (F.U.G.E.) had both refused to accept its ruling. In July 1961 a new Commission under Mr Guillebaud had recommended increases in salaries and allowances totalling $2.5 million. The report had been published in the September following. But although the government had accepted the findings in principle, they did nothing to implement them. Meetings between the government and the C.S.A. and F.U.G.E. became more tense in December and January, by the time the budget was put before the Legislative Assembly on January 31st, the government had so reduced morale, and so antagonised their own Service, that all grades were on the point of striking.

It was at this moment, that under the advice of Dr Nicholas Kaldor they produced a budget that was the toughest Guyana had known. There was little fundamentally wrong with the economics of the budget. If Guyana really wished to be

Refuge in Violence

independent then it had to begin to face reality and invest heavily in the infra-structure of new roads, large irrigation schemes and more rapid industrialization. Both the London *Times* and the *New York Times* commented favourably in these terms. There was no question of its being a pseudo-Communist budget, expropriating from the rich and letting the majority, as a vote catcher, get off lightly. It was, if anything exactly the opposite, rum, beer, cigarettes and other non-essential goods had increased taxes and new import duties were imposed to help the creation of local industries.

The only part that did effect both the rich and business people more strongly than the worker was the introduction of a 5% compulsory savings scheme, rising to 10%, that would be payable in bonds maturing in seven years.

It would not have been an easy budget for a government that had the confidence, or was accepted, by the majority of the people. Unfortunately for the P.P.P., it was neither of these. P.P.P. supporters were spread along a straggling coast road, but the opposition was firmly consolidated in the capital and had on its side the control and leadership of both the Civil Service and the trade unions.

The P.P.P. had not only manoeuvred into a position of weakness, but it had once again created a situation of 'all struggle and no unity'. Had it had the objectivity to analyse its own behaviour it would have seen that 'with true colonialist mentality', it had allowed itself to become obsessed by the need to produce a balanced budget at the cost of alienating its own Civil Service on which it relied for effective government.

d'Aguiar was quick to notice the weakness and to bring all his power to bear on the government. His paper, the *Chronicle*, and other anti-P.P.P. papers, the *Argosy* and *Post* came out with sensational headlines that grew with each day that passed more and more fiercely anti-government: 'Government to Squeeze Dollars from Workers'; 'Budget, It's Staggering'; 'Tax Avalanche will crush Working Class'; 'Slave Whip Budget.'

Letters to the editor began to suggest that people should fight to defend themselves and one letter in the *Chronicle*, only three days after the budget announcement, suggested that Burnham and d'Aguiar should both appear on the same platform . . . 'a general uprising against this budget . . . will force Jagan's government to either amend their ideas or resign'.

The P.P.P. accounts of the disasters that followed have tried to hide their mistakes behind the economic soundness of the budget, but they take no account of the strength of the feeling that their intransigence had created. As early as January 14th, Carl Blackman, editor of the Guyana *Sunday Graphic*, had predicted that there would be demonstrations during the three day visit by the Duke of Edinburgh to be held in February. Trouble was on the way and the budget gave the opposition the excuse they wanted.

On February 6th the Chamber of Commerce condemned it publicly. Shopkeepers had already begun to raise their prices, not only beyond the increase needed to meet the taxes that had not yet been applied, but also on goods that would not suffer increased taxation.

When the P.P.P. Ministers drove back into Georgetown with the Duke of Edinburgh, crowds lined the route booing and shouting at them, waving fists, and placards that told them to resign.

The first signs of the strength and seriousness of the situation came on Friday February 9th, when Dr. Jagan in the Legislative Assembly proposed the setting up of a Constitutional Committee in preparation for talks in London in the autumn on Guyana's independence.

The afternoon had begun in an uproar as 400 people crowded along the gallery outside the Chamber trying to find seats where there was room for only 118.

After Jagan had finished speaking, Burnham got up and roundly castigated both the proposals and the government. At the end he and his party rose and walked out, followed by most of the public. d'Aguiar then spoke and immediately he had finished, he and his party walked out. The government was left alone to themselves with only the shouts of angry crowds outside the building.

To preserve some face, the Attorney General seconded and

Refuge in Violence

spoke on the motion and then Dr Jagan stood up and announced that violence was being planned and attempts would be made on his life and the lives of his Ministers. Further that there was the intention to call a general strike on the next Monday and every effort was being made to bring the Civil Service out on strike.

He claimed that there was a small clique who wished to preserve their privileges and to create another Congo.

Subsequently a Commission of Inquiry comprising Sir Henry Wynn Parry from Britain, Sir Edward Asafu-Adjaye from Ghana, and Justice Gopal Das Khosla from India, made their report on the events that took place in the following week. They decided that there was no organized plot against the lives of the members of the Government, but merely an explosive situation that had been allowed to get out of hand.

Saturday was taken up by the T.U.C. in discussing whether or not they should call a general strike for Monday and finally deciding against it. The U.F. who did not hear of this decision until Sunday evening, spent nearly all the night trying to cancel their plans. Even so a number of people did not go to work and so were collected and formed into a demonstration. d'Aguiar led them past the Jagan's house (popularly known as the Red House, which also happened to be painted red) and Jack Kelshall's. They marched down Main Street, which led towards the business sector of the city. From here the demonstrators made their way to the public wireless station that the U.F. had dubbed 'Radio Moscow'.

On Tuesday afternoon, February 13th, a mass meeting was called by the T.U.C. as a demonstration of strength before they went to see the Finance Minister and discuss with him the budget. An hour before the meeting they learnt that the C.S.A. and F.U.G.E. had called their members out on strike. During the meeting, Richard Ishmael, President of the T.U.C. and the M.P.C.A., was told that Dr Jagan had just spoken on the wireless and announced that Civil Servants who did not return immediately would be dismissed. On the strength of this, he and other union leaders promptly called for a general strike. Although later in the day it was proved to him that the Premier had never made any such statement, the pot had by then boiled over and there was no going back.

The next day the Premier announced some modifications to the budget, but by then this was taken as a sign of weakness, d'Aguiar claimed that the government should resign: it was fortunate for him that they did not do so.

As well, the Governor, at the Premier's request, had issued a Proclamation banning meetings and gatherings within half a mile of the Public Buildings. The area included the Town Hall, the Victoria Law Courts, other government offices, Stabroek Market and part of the commercial buildings which made up the city's centre. This gave the opposition a chance to show publicly the strength they commanded in Georgetown. The next morning, Thursday, people began to gather around the proclaimed area. General opinion in Guyana is that this was largely at the instigation of d'Aguiar. Burnham finding himself being left behind as a popular leader, was forced to join in. d'Aguiar told the Commission that he happened to be there and was 'pressed' to join in.

While the Commission expressed doubts of his veracity on a number of other parts of his testimony, they accepted this statement and ascribed the initiative to Burnham. But it is probable that public opinion is more likely to be correct in saying that d'Aguiar was the initiator.

The two leaders marched side by side three times around the Public Buildings and then led the crowd to the P.N.C. headquarters. Here they publicly shook hands posing for photographs as they did so. The *Chronicle* reporting the demonstrations said of the two leaders, 'they shook hands, they embraced . . . their followers mingled. The mammoth crowd . . . moved on in face of dozens of fully armed Riot Squad policemen'. Memories of the past elections still rankled, but events had forced them to acknowledge that their only hope lay in working together. The P.P.P. had created against itself a united opposition.

Friday February 16th has gone down in Guyanese history as 'Black Friday'. In 1953, the P.P.P. had tried, by legislation, to make it possible to withdraw the Essential Services without the usual ten days notice. What they then failed to achieve, Richard Ishmael succeeded in doing as President of the T.U.C.

Refuge in Violence

On Friday morning he finally persuaded the Electricity workers to close down. The morning started with d'Aguiar addressing a crowd on the Parade Ground. The Parade Ground lay behind Government House, and along one corner the then P.N.C. headquarters stood. From the meeting, the crowd moved to the Power House to help persuade the 'scabs' that they should stop work. The police by this time were convinced that law and order was breaking down.

The Police Commissioner had attended a meeting with the Governor, the Premier and the Home Minister the evening before when the question of bringing in British troops had been discussed. The Governor, Sir Ralph Grey, had then told the Premier that as Guyana had full internal self-government he did not think that it was his duty to employ British troops to maintain in power a government that had obviously lost the confidence of a large section of the community. Only if it had become obvious that their own police force could not handle the situation would he come to the rescue. In other words he contended that it was their responsibility to govern by consent and not by British bayonets. The meeting was long and broke up with, it appears, differing understandings on what would happen. The Premier and Home Minister left believing that the British troops would at least be brought the twenty-five miles into Georgetown from Atkinson airfield, and kept in reserve. The Governor understood that he had promised that if the Prison Officers went on strike that evening, as had been rumoured, he would send for troops to take over the prisons. As the strike did not take place, the troops were not sent for.

When the police arrived at the Power Station on the Friday morning, they knew then that, as things stood, they were alone and it seemed time to show they would no longer countenance disorder. When the crowd refused to disperse, they used tear gas. People rushed into side alleys and then came pouring out again. With them was a woman carrying a young child. Immediately the cry went up that the police had killed the child, or it had died from the fumes. In fact it was taken to the hospital and quickly recovered.

d'Aguiar soon after this incident was addressing a crowd

outside his office; the soft-drinks factory stood across the street from the Public Buildings and d'Aguiar's own air-conditioned office was exactly opposite the Premier's. A note was brought to him saying that one or two children had died or been killed. He claims that he did not tell the crowd this, but said two children had been hurt and urged them to take this as an example not to resort to violence. The Commission did not accept this testimony and came to the conclusion that unable to resist the temptation d'Aguiar had encouraged the crowd in the belief that at least one child was dead.

The story lost nothing in the telling as it was carried around Georgetown. A blue Volkswagen touring the city asked people to go to the Parade Ground. And at 10.30 the electricity finally went off.

About 500 gathered at the Parade Ground and then moved off to attack the Headquarters of the P.P.P. in Robb Street. By this time they were extremely angry and two riot squads with about thirty men each tried to hold them back with tear gas as the crowd shouted, 'We are going to murder you, we are going to eat you, we are not going to disperse.'

A car was pushed towards the police and from behind it someone started to shoot at the police with an automatic .22. Superintendent McLeod was hit and subsequently died. Two other officers were also hit. The police fired back, taking care to aim at the car and not at the crowd. They hit one of the men who was pushing it, ironically enough, an early member of the P.P.P. who had been expelled for leftist-deviationism, and suddenly the shooting stopped.

By this time fires had begun to spread through the city – the first fire started when a car was turned over and set alight outside a row of Indian shops. Worse still electricity poles had been set alight, threatening the possibility of large areas of the city that would be in darkness that night, even if the men could be got back to work.

Almost all of Georgetown was then a city of wooden houses and flames spread rapidly. Without electricity it rapidly became impossible to maintain any pressure in the mains and the Fire Brigade had to rely on its few water tenders and the canals. The crowds did all they could to hinder the Fire

Refuge in Violence

Brigade in their work, cutting and stealing the hoses and by the end of the day over 4,000 feet had been damaged or lost. Also at one time during the day the Fire Brigade was fired on.

With the ever increasing violence near the P.P.P. headquarters and the rapidly spreading fires, the Police Commissioner called for military aid. By half past two in the afternoon, the first troops had arrived. Gradually throughout the afternoon order was restored, but the price was heavy. Fifty-six business premises had been burnt out, another twenty-one had been damaged and sixty-six had been both damaged and looted: the centre of Georgetown was a smouldering ruin. Nobody has ever estimated how much in terms of money this cost. Relatively few people were insured against civil commotion and riot, but those that were, presented claims for over £2 million.

What follows was an uneasy truce. The P.P.P. learnt very little, if anything, from the experience. The opposition parties and the T.U.C. believed that they had been on the point of toppling the government and they had seen, much to their surprise, what power they could command. This they remembered.

Chapter 20

A SECOND CHANCE

AFTER the Georgetown riots the P.P.P. was faced with two ugly problems that it would have preferred not to think about.

The first was that each Constitutional advance had given it, as a party in power, greater responsibility and therefore a greater interest in law and order. Should it give up its so-called 'revolutionary' attitude and restrict itself to the legislative powers that it had, or should it persist in trying to maintain politics at boiling point by such party manoeuvres as trying to capture the trade unions?

The former demanded a completely fresh analysis of its position, similar to the one propounded by Dr Jagan in 1956. But the P.P.P. had since shown itself to be temperamentally incapable of implementing this policy. Was it any better equipped now? Those in favour of maintaining the old tactics argued that even if these created discord and were in the short-term advantageous to the opposition, they would prove in the long-run to be the only way that the party could hold onto power.

The second arose because the P.P.P. had no option but to run its government from Georgetown, the centre of its administration and of the commercial life of the country. But Georgetown was enemy territory, where their every action could be answered by mass demonstrations. Should they try to placate and divide some of the enemies, or should they continue to try to dominate them? Georgetown was used by those who believe in 'revolution' as the typical example of how useless it was to try to follow a policy of moderation.

A Second Chance

The opposition had already gained the initiative, to try to placate them would be taken as a sign of weakness.

The summer passed quietly, while these two problems, in one form or another, came up for discussion but were never resolved.

So it was that by the autumn, when the three political parties went to London to put forward recommendations for a new Constitution, under which independence would be granted, the P.P.P. found itself once again faced by united opposition. The talks opened at Lancaster House on October 23rd and eighteen sessions later, on November 6th, they closed with nothing of any importance decided.

The P.P.P. had drafted a constitution for a republican government within the Commonwealth, comprising an executive council of ministers and a single chamber legislature. At the other extreme was the U.F. who wanted a monarchical form of government. Fundamental as these differences were, the real point of disagreement had come over the franchise. The P.P.P., with its rapidly increasing Indian population, wanted the franchise extended from twenty-one years of age to eighteen and although this would have made it virtually certain that the P.P.P. would win, it had also, quite naturally, said that it did not want to go to the polls again before independence.

The P.N.C. and the U.F. were determined that the voting age should not be lowered and they wanted proportional representation with a single nationwide constituency to take advantage of their united majority of votes. As well, they wanted elections before independence.

The P.P.P. had gone to the talks expecting that whatever else happened a firm date for independence would be set. When he did not get this, Dr Jagan decided to force through the Party Executive the policy of trying to create a national front. He demanded, and obtained, permission to open talks with the P.N.C. on the possible formation of a coalition. He argued that it would drive a wedge between the P.N.C. and the U.F. and, probably, the trade unions as well.

The permission was granted most unwillingly, as many people believed that from 1956 Dr Jagan had shown himself more interested in maintaining his own position than in the ideology of his party. Once engaged in talks with the P.N.C. would these opportunist tendencies lead him, and therefore the party, into a coalition that it did not need, and destroy for ever its chance to be the vanguard party of the masses? Personal animosities, and a natural reluctance to share with others the limited positions of power, also played their part in this attitude.

The tactics that had proved so successful for dealing with inter-party differences from 1953 onwards were employed once again to ensure the failure of the talks. The newspapers obtained inside information on what the party had decided and rumours, as well as quotations supposedly made by Jagan about Burnham, were circulated freely.

The first move for the talks took place in December 1962. But it was not until nearly the end of March 1963, that the first meeting between Jagan and Burnham took place and by that time the policy of a national front had become officially discredited within the P.P.P. Jagan, whose own ambivalence had helped make this possible, could only keep the talks going by writing to Burnham suggesting that the P.P.P. and P.N.C. each put a three man team to discuss points of agreement. The P.P.P. team comprised Ashton Chase (Leader of the Senate), Ranji Chandisingh (Ministry of Labour, Health and Housing) and Moses Bhagwan, who under Brindley Benn led the militant Progressive Youth Organization. Other events had anyway made the national front policy impossible to put through, but the composition of the P.P.P. team was guaranteed to prevent any agreement being reached.

The P.P.P. extremists had decided to renew their attack on the trade unions. On February 16th and 17th, they called the first Congress of the Guiana Sugar Workers' Union. At the Congress they changed the name to Guiana Agricultural Workers' Union (G.A.W.U.), but the initials, and in everything else, it was strongly reminiscent of the G.I.W.U. of the past that was meant to capture the Indian fieldworkers from the M.P.C.A.

Richard Ishmael, as President of the M.P.C.A. reacted immediately and called out the sugar workers to prove that

A Second Chance

he had control of them still. On the first day, Tuesday March 5th, eight estates were out, by the next day, the rest followed. Having made his point, he called off the strike the same evening and agreed to open conciliatory talks.

In March, Burnham staged an unemployment march through Georgetown and at the same time the P.P.P. picketed Government House with placards stating that the British, and not they, were responsible for the situation. Violence was getting near again as one could see from the party bodyguards who hovered around expectantly.

When the P.P.P. suddenly published a Labour Relations Bill, that hardly differed in text, and not at all in spirit, from the 1953 Bill, everyone knew that a show-down was both imminent and inescapable.

The P.P.P. had made the same mistake as in 1953 of publishing the Bill before entering into discussions with the interested parties. Four days later on March 29th, Ranji Chandisingh told the T.U.C. that he was prepared to meet them and did not intend to rush the Bill through. But everyone recognized the tactics. Any concessions the P.P.P. now made would be a public step-down and it could not therefore be expected to make any essential changes.

There were protests and meetings and now it was not merely the pattern of 1953 that was being repeated but also that of the year before. The staffing problems at the Rice Marketing Board had caused disturbances and on a number of occasions the police had had to be called in to help keep order. On Friday April 5th – another 'Black Friday – pro-union workers who had been running a 'go slow movement' were locked out and threatened with dismissal. They tried to break their way in, aided by an excited crowd, and had to be dispersed by the use of tear gas. The crowd became angry and moved down Water Street looting and breaking into shops. Looting also broke out in other parts of the city. The result of the night's violence was one dead, several wounded and an estimated loss of £20,000.

But it was not to be the end of violence, for the very next day shops and municipal markets had to close down threatened by further looting and hooliganism. The three political leaders piously condemned the violence and events continued along the same course as before.

The publication of the Bill prevented the government from withdrawing it and the same time gave the opposition the chance to arouse public feeling. The extremist element in the P.P.P. had successfully put through its policy of having a show-down that no amount of coalition talks could cancel.

The policy, however, had not been arrived at by logical analysis or calm thought. Those who were responsible for it could give no clear reasons why they believed it would be successful, but to them after months of party wrangling this, for the moment, ended the internal party strife and gave the leadership back to them. The only point the P.P.P. hung on to with certainty was that after the Black Friday of the year before the British Government would be bound to support them with troops, otherwise, they believed, it would be condemned in the eyes of the world for allowing lives and property to be sacrificed for political considerations. At the worst, said the extremists we will be forced into opposition, and then we will turn the strike weapon against any government that comes to power, or failing that we will take to the forests and lead a guerilla movement. It was heady talk.

So although negotiations went on while the Bill began its course in the Legislative Assembly, it was obvious that the differences could not be resolved by discussion.

The C.S.A. and F.U.G.E., the two Civil Service Unions, stood by the T.U.C. and when on April 18th, a general strike call was sent out, they both agreed to join. So on Saturday, April 20th the second general strike in Guyana's history started. It was to go on for 80 days to be probably the longest in world history.

On May 9th, the Governor declared a State of Emergency, but the opposition realised that they had to play this very slowly. If the people of Georgetown broke loose immediately, the British troops would be brought in and that would probably mean the end of the strike. Passive resistance became the theme, with violence always around the corner. On May 20th, the thirty-third day of the strike, the first "Freedom Riders" appeared in the streets. These were groups of people on

A Second Chance

bicycles riding pell-mell along the almost empty roads since there was hardly any petrol for cars. They were followed, ignominiously, by the police in vans. But bicycles gave them a freedom of movement that the police found difficult to cope with. A large group followed by the police would suddenly break into two, cycling off in different directions. Whichever the police followed would lead them away from the commercial area and gradually disintegrate, until it was not worth following. The other in the meantime had doubled back into the shopping areas and was busily engaged in closing down shops.

The Governor at the request of the Premier had declared the first State of Emergency under his powers for fourteen days. It could either be extended by him or by the Legislative Assembly. The P.P.P. naturally did not want to be seen as hiding behind his coat-tails and on May 20th introduced a motion for its extension. It had three clear parliamentary days to pass this. With an ineptitude that particularly reflected the failure to plan ahead of the extremist element, Brindley Benn, as Leader of the House, allowed his party members speeches of sometimes an hour or even two. It was only when the last day came, that he realized that the opposition who had also been making long speeches still had a number of members who had not spoken. An attempt was made to apply the guillotine, but this could not be reached by inter-party agreement as already P.P.P. members had had so much time allowed to them. It had to be done by using the P.P.P. majority, necessitating counts and recounts that all took up precious minutes.

If the Bill were not passed by midnight they would have to call on the Governor to get them out of the mess by using his powers. By 11.45 it seemed likely that they could get the closure and vote before midnight, at that moment W. O. R. Kendall, deputy leader of the P.N.C. proposed an amendment, Burnham seconded him, precious minutes went by as Benn stood up to ask the Speaker to rule it out of order. At a few minutes before midnight the Speaker allowed the amendment, and minutes later while Burnham was still speaking on it, midnight arrived and the Bill had not been passed.

Trouble in Guyana

Dr Jagan and five other Members of the government were so incensed that they left before the Speaker and as he passed through the lobby with the Mace carried before him, they called him an 'Imperialist stooge' and many other unflattering words. The most unflattering, however, was an action by a P.P.P. member, Mohammed Saffee, that translated into words obviously meant 'Balls to You'. Press photographers were in the lobby and this made the front page photograph of the next day. The Premier and other members were suspended until they apologized.

The House next met five days later and Dr Jagan and his colleagues refused to leave when ordered to do so. They appealed against the ruling to the Chief Justice, but the Chief Justice refused to give judgement on an action of the Speaker in the Legislative body.

Without the the five members the P.P.P. no longer had a majority and when in June, d'Aguiar tried to introduce a no-confidence motion, the Mace was found to be missing having been handed over to the Premier. The Deputy Clerk of the House said he had been afraid it was no longer safe in the Public Buildings. Why he had not handed it to the Speaker he did not make clear. Eventually faced with having to apologise or lose the P.P.P. majority in the House, Dr Jagan was forced to call on the Governor to prorogue the Assembly, although in doing so the Labour Relations Bill, which had not passed through all its stages, was also annulled.

The strike was punctuated by occasional outbursts of violence: acid bombs were thrown at well-known political supporters, and dynamite was found under the Rice Marketing Board on more than one occasion. There was the constant fear that the petrol storage tanks up river would be damaged on an ebb-tide and the petrol ignited as it reached the wooden dock front of the city. Bombs were placed in government offices and nobody from the political and trade union leaders downwards felt safe.

Finally, on July 7th, when it had become obvious to both sides that they had reached a stalemate, the eighty day strike ended, with promises on the government side of no victimization, especially against the Civil Service, and an agreement

A Second Chance

to discuss with representatives of the unions and the employers any future Labour Relations Bill.

Mr Duncan Sandys, who was then British Secretary of State for the Colonies, came out to Guyana and exhorted all parties to come together. He took great pleasure in visiting different villages and making an Indian and Negro shake hands and be photographed. The futility of this action and the series of platitudes put forward at the end of the visit were not lost on the Guyanese. Jagan and the P.P.P. could hope for little support from London when they went there again in the autumn to discuss once more the question of a new constitution and independence.

Once again Lancaster House was the scene for their deliberations. The first meeting started on October 22nd and Sandys inquired whether they had reached any agreement. When they said they had not, he proposed that there should be further private talks both with him and between the leaders themselves. The deadlock remained until Dr Jagan came up with the amazing proposal that Sandys should provide a solution. Nobody else could quite believe what they heard.

Even more improbably, Dr Jagan agreed when Sandys suggested it that Sandys might draft the letter for the three leaders to sign. It was with open-eyed incredulity that P.N.C. and U.F. later watched Dr. Jagan sign this letter which read:

'At your request we have made further efforts to resolve the differences between us on the constitutional issues which require to be settled before British Guiana secures independence, in particular, the electoral system, the voting age, and the question whether fresh elections should be held before independence.

We regret to have to report to you that we have not succeeded in reaching agreement; and we have reluctantly come to the conclusion that there is no prospect of an agreed solution. Another adjournment of the Conference for further discussions between ourselves would therefore serve no useful purpose and would result only in further delaying British

Guiana's independence and in continued uncertainty in the country.

In these circumstances we are agreed to ask the British Government to settle on their authority all outstanding constitutional issues, and we undertake to accept their decisions.'

With his signature Dr Jagan threw away the gains that he had made over more than a decade and a half: from the time when he and Burnham stood up before the Waddington Commission and told them that all the Commission needed to do was to recommend universal suffrage to elect a Constituent Assembly.

In the first paragraph, Dr Jagan conceded that there could be the possibility of fresh elections before independence. In the last he gave the British Government full authority to settle all issues and bound himself to follow them. When the news reached Guyana, the P.P.P. was horror-struck. When the news of the settlement itself came through they at first found it impossible to believe that their leader could have led them into such a commitment.

Sandys' solution gave everything to the opposition, proportional representation, one constituency, no reduction in the voting age and elections to be held in the near future, without, however, even conceding a date for independence.

Burnham could not believe that he would get away with such a gift. When Jagan, on hearing the solution, left yelling 'treachery', Burnham followed in the same vein and blamed Jagan for having sold their birthright. His own P.N.C. had welcomed the news with triumph, but as the statements by the two leaders came in over the wire services they were thrown into complete confusion and did not know whether to celebrate what was so obviously to their advantage or cast aspersions, with their leader, that were just as obviously undeserved. Burnham lived down his mistake by silence. Dr Jagan compounded his with words.

Jagan returned on the morning of November 10th, he spoke only a few sentences at the airport and left immediately for P.P.P. headquarters. There on the top floor with about 300

A Second Chance

people crowded in he started to lambast Sandys and the British. He did not, however, explain why he had given them full powers. The meeting was obviously dragging and confusion was becoming even greater when Jocelyn Hubbard came to the rescue by shouting 'Cuba Si, Britain No'. This irrelevance was well-timed. The stalwarts took it up and the meeting at least ended with united shouting, if not in general comprehension of why things had gone wrong.

There were those in the party leadership who were not averse to Dr Jagan compromising himself still further while, in his angry mood, leading the party further along the path of revolutionary struggle. They therefore agreed when he said he would go out that afternoon to address the Progressive Youth Congress. Political wisdom at that moment might have suggested silence, or at the most a blanket statement, until he knew more about the reaction in the country and, with his Party, had had time to work out a new policy.

Instead, having reviewed a march past of uniformed P.Y.O.'s conspicuously led by those who had recently returned from Cuba, he spoke first of British perfidy and then of the great achievements of Fidel Castro.

If necessary, he, Jagan, would emulate Castro and go into the hills. It was quite a long speech, but there was more fantasy than policy and observers from Cuba and Communist delegates were not impressed.

Eight days later the P.P.P. organized sixteen rallies along the coastal belt calling on the people to defy the gross imposition. For the moment there was little else they could do.

In December, Bridley Benn, as Chairman of the P.P.P., on a visit to Ghana proposed that the Ghanaians should send a delegation to observe and make recommendations. Ghana until this time had been firmly behind the P.P.P. which it had considered the most progressive of all the parties. It was therefore easily agreed that their United Nations representative, Mr Quaison-Sackey, should spend five days in British Guiana in January to see what kind of a mission would be most suitable. He had talks with Burnham and won agreement for the mission. He then left without commenting, but

Trouble in Guyana

as was to be subsequently proved, extremely disturbed by what he had found.

The arrival of the mission from Ghana coincided with a gigantic 'Freedom March' that had been organized by Brindley Benn while the Jagans were away in Jamaica attending a Caribbean Conference.

On this culminating day, thousands of Indians converged on Georgetown. Those who had entered from the west marched through deserted streets. There was not a sound to meet them, except the padding of their bare feet. Their long dark, melancholy eyes looked a little apprehensively around as they went further and further into the Negro stronghold. But both Burnham and d'Aguiar had again shown their command in Georgetown. They had told their followers they must ignore the procession as this was the only way to make it insignificant.

What was not insignificant was the impression these long lines of P.P.P. supporters created on the Ghanaian mission. P.P.P. leadership and Ministers had a high proportion of Negroes, but as the procession marched past the hotel where the Ghanaians stood they could see that 99% of the P.P.P. supporters were Indians.

When the talks took place, designed to find common ground between the P.P.P. and the P.N.C., the Ghanaians were struck again and again by the intransigence of the P.P.P. members and the willingness of Burnham and the P.N.C. to listen to what they had to say. When the Mission left it had the firm impression that the problem in Guyana had a racial basis and their African government was backing an Indian party.

Meanwhile, in January, the G.A.W.U. (a sugar workers union) was told by the P.P.P. extremists to step up their fight for recognition. Cane fires broke out and a month later, the S.P.A. announced that 698 acres had been destroyed, worth more than a million dollars. With it came strikes, intimidation and violence. Indians and Negroes who had lived in the villages together for years, suddenly found themselves in a state of siege. Minorities had to move from one village, usually leaving everything they possessed behind, to another where they were in a majority. Houses were set fire to, others small

A Second Chance

and pathetic were pushed off their long stilts and toppled to the ground. Often with the terrified owners still inside them.

The newspapers throughout 1964 hardly have a day without some incident. Frequently for three or four days running the stories of violence are so ghastly that they took precedence over everything else.

On May 22nd a State of Emergency was declared and on June 12th Arthur Abraham and seven of his children were burnt to death in their house. Abraham, a senior civil servant, had been Secretary to the Premier. His family were staunch United Force supporters.

The next day, the Governor Sir Richard Luyt, who had arrived in March, ordered the detention of thirty-two persons: these included Brindley Benn, Moses Bhagwan, Harry Lall (President of the G.A.W.U.), Victor Downer (P.P.P. member of the Legislature), 'Fireball' Philomena Sahoye (Secretary of the G.A.W.U.), other members of the P.P.P. and some P.N.C.

By then the G.A.W.U. strike had lasted 125 days and some forty-three deaths were attributable to it. The violence continued until the elections on December 7th and then died out.

When the votes came to be counted, P.P.P. had increased their percentage to 45.83 and so gained twenty-four seats, the P.N.C. had dropped 0.4% and the U.F. had lost nearly 4%. But the P.N.C. and the U.F. had won twenty-two seats and seven respectively, which, if they formed a coalition would make twenty-nine seats. The other parties that had been formed in the hope that under proportional representation they might have a chance did not collect one percent of the votes and joined the shadows of other hopeless causes.

The elections showed that once again people had voted race. The difference this time was that, under proportional representation, the Indians had become a minority. What did this mean for the future?

Chapter 21

POINTS OF DEPARTURE

It was a wet Sunday evening on December 13th when the Governor called Forbes Burnham to the Residency and asked him to form a government. Both of them must have realised that they were making history and both must have wondered how posterity would judge them. During the past year over 200 men, women, and children had died violent deaths and in many parts of the country a state of smouldering civil war still existed. It only needed a small incident for it to break out once more and for the cry to go up that the 'Negro menace' had now become a legalized entity.

Dr Jagan had not helped to make the transfer of power any easier and he was later to do all that he could to spread dissatisfaction and fear of the P.N.C.

As his party had won the largest number of seats, he was the first to be invited to form a government. In a desperate attempt to reverse his former policy and retain power, he went to Burnham and offered him the premiership with equal representation for the P.N.C. in the Council of Ministers. It was, however, too late. Burnham, who knew that he could work with the U.F., gave a flat refusal.

Unable to form a coalition government, Dr Jagan then tried, having contested the elections, to impugn their validity and refused to offer his resignation. An Order-in-Council had to be signed by the Queen to remove him and his Ministers from the positions of power that they no longer exercised.

As a last official act, a number of P.P.P. Ministers returned to their offices and smoke began to rise from bonfires started in the enclosures behind them. It was widely said that

Points of Departure

embarrassing files and minutes were being turned to ashes. The other suggestion put forward was that, as they cleared their desks, they felt cold.

A week later, the P.P.P. began a series of country-wide rallies with the theme, 'We were cheated, not defeated', but after three years of turmoil, strikes, violence and personal sacrifice there was little response from the people and much criticism.

It was then that Dr Jagan found the mistakes of the past were about to take their toll. He had retained control of the party only because he could command mass support. When it became obvious that this was no longer effective, those who had for some time viewed his constant changes of policy with increasing concern decided that it was time that they stepped forward. A battle for the leadership was about to begin.

If there is any moment in time that one can put one's finger on and say, 'It started there', it must be the moment when Dr Jagan decided to go out to address the P.Y.O. Congress in November 1963 and commit himself publicly to a policy of extreme militancy. From this moment came the decision to call countrywide protest meetings, and from this moment the decision to boycott the elections and to refuse to resign. This could have been a viable policy, but it called for more than Dr Jagan was prepared to pay.

His friends abroad pointed out that if the P.P.P. boycotted the elections it would be tantamount to admitting that they were a purely Indian party without any general support and, worse still, that far from being a broad national front movement, they had so alienated the non-Indian electorate that no other party would even consider working in a coalition with them.

Both Dr and Mrs Jagan saw the wisdom of this comment and decided to change their policy. In doing so they threw over the militant group whose policies they had been supporting, and turned back to the more moderate group whom they had earlier so brusquely discarded. They put the argument to the Executive for approval. At the same time they presented a list of candidates for December. As the elections were to be held under P.R. those near the top of the list stood the greatest chance of being elected. The Executive immediately noticed that the names of religious leaders and prominent middle-class supporters occupied a number of these places, while others and more left-wing supporters were placed below them. This created an immediate uproar. The Jagan argument that these candidates could easily be controlled by the Marxist leadership, did little to placate those Marxists who now wondered whether Dr Jagan was interested in anything at all beyond retaining his power at any price.

The divisions within the leadership crystallized about three people, Brindley Benn, a Negro, and Chairman of the Party, Moses Bhagwan, an Indian, and leader of the Progressive Youth Organization (P.Y.O.); and lastly, Ashton Chase, also a Negro and one of the founder members.

Benn, with that intemperence that often characterises those who are accused of having betrayed their own people, continued to advocate the boycott of the elections and tougher measures in the sugar strike, a policy that would eventually lead to armed struggle and a state of civil war. Benn found little support except among those who felt their position insecure and were prepared to accept any means to remain in power.

Moses Bhagwan saw that the P.P.P. had virtually no chance of winning the election alone and no allies to whom it could turn. He therefore argued that the P.P.P. should cease to be a national front movement, and should instead be a vanguard party; a party that based its policy on purely Marxist lines, that organized itself as a Communist Party, with both an overt and secret membership, and one that applied Party discipline to its members.

To Bhagwan, this seemed to be the only way that the party could break free from its racial background. Also it would be able to create the discipline in its leadership and followers that would enable it to withstand any attack that might be launched against it. This policy, he knew, might well lead to an armed struggle. It was not, however, the same as Benn's policy advocating the use of an undisciplined 'bourgeois' party to support Marxist ideals. This if one looked at it realistically came down to a straight fight between the Indians and Negroes. Bhagwan however hoped to go into the struggle with a small but highly disciplined party with support both among the Negro in the towns and the Indians in the countryside.

The third candidate was Ashton Chase. Chase was put forward by those who feared, for different reasons, that either Benn or Bhagwan might dominate the party. Some thought that Benn's supporters were too powerful and too erratic; others that Benn was a liability who did not command any Negro votes. While Chase, who was gentler and with the skill of an old trade unionist, might be able to attract some of the Negro votes, as well as, at the least, neutralise some of the unions. Religion also came into it. Some of the Indian Moslem party leaders described Benn as irreligious and a menace.

It was in this way that Dr Jagan entered 1965. He had no clear policy on his own part and his party leadership was divided between three groups. As in the past, he had neither the machinery, nor the will, to settle the differences.

He and the contestants, instead of trying to work towards a solution, began to plan their annual trips abroad where they hoped to canvass sucessfully their own personal views and to obtain support among the Communist parties of the countries they visited.

Moses Bhagwan visited Britain, China, Hungary and Cuba, as well as attending a meeting of the World Federation of Democratic Youth in Ghana and the Preparatory Committee of the World Peace Council in Belgium. He made no secret of the differences that existed in the P.P.P., nor of his own analysis of the party's position. He returned as the officially recognized representative of the New China News Agency (N.C.N.A.). This appointment, which had formerly been assigned to the *Mirror*, the P.P.P. newspaper, made everyone wonder whether it now carried with it the official blessing for Bhagwan's views of the Chinese Communist Party.

Brindley Benn chose Africa and China, but came back with no obvious blessing from anyone but with some additional funds.

Dr Jagan, after a visit to London to put forward his case to his friends there, went to Czechoslovakia, Hungary, East Germany and Cuba.

Dr Jagan returned just as the explosion within the party was about to take place. But, as on previous occasions, he gave himself no time in which he could rectify earlier mistakes and so anticipate events. It was Good Friday when he returned and on the next day the P.P.P. Congress opened. The fight for the Chairmanship of the Party would once again be on and Benn's supporters had made it clear that if he were not re-elected they would resort to violence. Dr Jagan had to decide whether it were better to break with Benn or confirm him in his position. He tried instead to avoid the issue.

It cannot have been an easy meeting for Dr Jagan to attend. He had nothing to offer but bad news, and he knew that the control was slipping through his fingers. In the beginning of his speech he threatened Mohamed Saffee with disciplinary action for attending sessions of the House of Assembly which the P.P.P. was boycotting. He then went on to announce that once the motion on the Budget had been passed, the P.P.P. would end the boycott and attend the Assembly. He did not attempt to explain why this decision had been taken.

There had been two reasons for the boycott. One that was made public and one that was secret. The public reason was that the P.P.P. did not consider the elections valid, but when Dr Jagan announced the end of the boycott he did not say whether this meant that the P.P.P. now recognized the elections. The secret reason was the split within the party: Dr Jagan had felt it wiser for neither Benn nor Bhagwan to have an opportunity to speak for the party in parliament while he was away. Both the reasons for the boycott, and the threat of disciplinary action against Mohamed Saffee, were never properly explained to the Congress.

Dr Jagan, then went on to say that it was therefore impossible to hold party elections and instead he proposed nominating an 'Administrative Council' headed by himself. It would include the former Chairman (Brindley Benn) and have representatives from the P.Y.O., the Women's Progressive Organization (W.P.O.) and the G.A.W.U. (the pro-P.P.P. sugar workers' union).

Points of Departure

By the time the Congress ended, Dr Jagan had shown that he was no longer in control but despite this was desperately trying to hold onto the strings of power. To those who knew what was going on, it was clear that the Jagans expected another split. The only question that was left open was whether Bhagwan would precede Benn, or Benn, Bhagwan.

In July of 1965, Moses Bhagwan was suspended. In August he was forced to resign. With him went 12 members of the P.Y.O. but Jagan calmly announced that the P.Y.O., on Bhagwan's own estimate, had 14,000 members, so 12 resignations presented no threat.

There were bitter public recriminations and 'leaks' to the press. The *Sunday Chronicle* reported that soon afterwards Bhagwan allegedly warned Mrs Jagan that she should stop attacking him personally as one of the 'cowards' who had left the party to 'hang their mouths whene the soup was falling', since she herself was 'an open target'. Bhagwan allegedly stated, 'Mrs Janet Jagan whose reactions during the 1962–1964 violent upheavals are well known to some of us; Mrs Janet Jagan who was on the verge of quitting Guiana on several occasions and who, instead of former Treasurer Mr Ramkarran, personally controlled and disbursed the millions of dollars in the P.P.P. Treasury, should refrain from accusing any person, particularly a group of Guyanese politicians, of cowardice, of quitting a struggle and of hanging their mouths where the soup falls'. As a footnote, it is only fair to add that so far as I know, Mrs Jagan never showed fear during the times of violence – if anything it was the opposite.

As the book goes to press, Brindley Benn is still in the party, but his group is said to have had a meeting with Jagan and the rift was so great that the meeting broke up prematurely. Mr Benn has also made no secret of his views on Mrs Jagan and has not hesitated to use racial arguments in his attack.

It is a sad decline from former days. The P.P.P. that was once the most progressive radical party in the country, now hangs back: when an Independence Conference was proposed for November 1965, it was Dr Jagan who decided that the P.P.P. would boycott it. It is ironic that the P.P.P. should now be trying so hard to return to the past, and for it to be working for Guyana to remain a colony.

One former Guyanese politician recently commented: 'It is indeed very sad to watch a man commit political hari-kiri so many times in a few years. On each occasion Jagan was given the opportunity to do something for his country, his fellow Indians, or, in the narrower view, at least for his party. Men who were unknown in the forties and early fifties, when Jagan was already internationally famous, have since led their countries to independence. But Jagan has only led us into trouble. Sometimes I think that more than anything else, Jagan brought us trouble.'

Before leaving the P.P.P. it is worth asking what brought about this decline in the fortunes of the Jagans and their party.

Dr Jagan's answer is that it was the Machiavellian act of Duncan Sandys who, in order to get rid of him, introduced an inferior electoral system to the one Guyana already had. A number of people, aware of the disadvantages of proportional representation, were at first prepared to accept Dr Jagan's argument. Subsequent events have shown that this was an over-simplification that did not take into account the conditions ruling in the P.P.P. leadership, nor the historical events that had led up to 1963.

The greatest disadvantage inherent in proportional representation is that frequently no party obtains a clear cut majority. The government that is subsequently formed comes about by a coalition of two or more parties and must therefore constantly attend to minority interests. But was this such a bad thing in Guyana? For over a decade the P.P.P. had, under first past the post, been elected and had used its constitutional powers to disregard the wishes of the rest of the electorate. This had meant that over half of the voting population was virtually disenfranchised. As they watched one election follow another, they came to see that they had no means of influencing the P.P.P. by constitutional methods. They therefore resorted to demonstrations and strikes that, as the years went by, became a threat to law and order and led to ever increasing violence. They had an historical precedent: these were

Points of Departure

exactly the tactics that Dr Jagan had employed against the British when he was in a similarly weak position constitutionally

One is left wondering whether proportional representation that has made Forbes Burnham consider the interests of all the different communities, was really an inferior electoral system at that time in Guyana's history.

There is one more point that was clearly brought out by the dissension in the P.P.P. leadership. Dr Jagan maintained that P.R. was designed to get rid of him. But he forgot that he, as the other political leaders, had a year in which to mend his political fences. It was probable, as indeed happened, that his party would poll the largest number of votes. It was therefore possible that he would lead the next coalition government. Was it not also possible for him to put his own house in order and gather about him the broad national front that he claimed his party represented?

Before one can answer this, one must turn to the few months in which Forbes Burnham has governed the country.

Even those who knew Burnham well wondered what kind of a Prime Minister he would make. While in opposition one of his dominant traits was an indolence that often goes with genius. But what *was* his genius? It could well have been only as a courtroom lawyer, or as a smart politician. He had an ability to think on his feet, and to think more trenchantly and more wittily than anyone who opposed him. As a result in parliament, or at public meetings, even his enemies could enjoy his speeches, his humour, and his quick ripostes. But both friend and enemy alike were left afterwards trying to find any underlying policy or loyalty to principle.

What actually happened came as a surprise to both friend and opponent. Overnight he grew in stature and became a statesman. Under Jagan the office of Prime Minister was a post to be denigrated as a gift from the colonialists – a mere appendage to party leadership. But under Burnham it became the centre of a policy-making government and administration. Dr Jagan's hours in his office were frequently cut short by other business, under Burnham the lights burn late while he tries to introduce order and system into the government, and to create a new unity of Guyanese ambitions and aspirations.

How many of these objectives Burnham will be able to realize, in the five years his government has to run, cannot be estimated. He came to a country that was almost bankrupt, whose governmental machinery was so run down that it could no longer work effectively. He took over a country that was divided racially, professionally and socially.

But some of these legacies from the days when the P.P.P. failed to rule could prove invaluable assets.

In the Civil Service there were more than 500 professional and technical posts vacant. A relic of the bitter enmity felt by the P.P.P. for its own Civil Service and its acceptance of the colonialist requirements that Budgets should be balanced. In the Ministry of Works and Hydraulics alone, a vital Ministry in a country of canals and dykes, there were over 170 vacancies. Burnham has said that employment of only one additional architect will provide permanent work for 500 people.

So the P.P.P. gave Burnham the opportunity to offer expatriate Guyanese good employment back at home, to provide work for the better educated and to provide new employment for the working classes.

Unemployment when he took over stood at the phenomenal figure of 20% of the labour force – more than 40,000 people. Under-employment was impossible to estimate. Within six months Burnham announced that the Labour Exchange had placed 6,000 people, which was more than in the previous two years under the P.P.P.

There are now plans to 'de-colonize' the sugar plantations. Selling off the land to workers while leaving for the moment the factories and distribution in the hands of the sugar companies.

It is when one gets these problems, that one begins to see the difficulties ahead. Owner production of cane will be less efficient than plantation methods. The choice, however, is not a simple one. Plantations cannot employ the full labour force they require at certain periods throughout the whole year.

Points of Departure

Under-employment has in the past been concomitant with efficiency.

It is too early even to diagnose the many problems that have been hidden during the last decade.

Guyana can only develop at a certain, but unknown rate. On the one side is the need to find employment for thousands of people, on the other is the need to get the economy moving. An example of this is the necessity to surface and improve the 300 mile road system. Burnham had to choose between importing machinery and doing the work quickly, or doing it slowly, and expensively, with a large labour force. He could solve one of the problems, but not both. He chose machinery and was castigated by Dr Jagan, who had forgotten that it was he who left the roads unsurfaced and he who did not give the people work.

But of the problems that face Burnham and his government the greatest is the need to win the trust and participation of the Indian community. No one at present can say whether or not he will succeed. But, at least, the violence and the bloodshed is, for the moment, at an end.

Even if it is still too soon to judge Burnham as a premier, one cannot forget that his first government has lasted for more than 133 days. He has tried to govern, which Dr Jagan never tried to do, and he has shown that he is not afraid to employ men who have the qualifications for the posts they hold. Under Dr Jagan, the Planning Department gradually fell to pieces and those who had any interest in building a new society left completely disillusioned. Burnham has appointed Sir Arthur Lewis, a Guyanese who was formerly at Manchester and Princeton University, to draft a Five Year Plan. He chose one of the best qualified Guyanese lawyers, 'Sonny' Ramphal, an Indian who had practised in Jamaica for many years, as his Attorney General. He has been prepared to compromise with the U.F. in order to bring the country together and produce, for once, a viable economy that will underpin an independent Guyana.

When one looks back it is difficult to see what Dr Jagan thought he was doing. His first, and every subsequent entry into trade union politics was disastrous. He, if any one, is responsible for their present concern over political rather than trade union matters, and ironically enough it is they who oppose him so strongly.

He began well, even bravely, in the Legislative Council. but when the riots and deaths at Enmore gave him a chance to come to power, he forgot both that and his promise to Burnham.

He was given an overwhelming majority in 1953 but led his party into the fantasy that they were 'in opposition', so that they never looked beyond the narrow requirements of party politics, as they saw them, to the great challenge of leading a nation to independence.

Far back in 1947, P.A.C. discussed whether it should take power by legal means or by armed revolt. It was never resolved and this question, eighteen years later, has just split his party into at least three different factions.

At one time he had behind him some of the greatest personalities in the Labour Party in Britain. But he chose to scorn their advice of slow, but certain, progress so that today he has boycotted the meeting that will give Guyana her independence.

His charm, his personality, his ability to speak to people as one of themselves, overcame every Indian party that was set up against him. In a few years he had won such recognition from his people that when, after the suspension of the constitution, the British government and sugar companies financed new housing developments and raised salaries, it was Cheddi Jagan who got the credit. For the decade that he was in Guyanese politics, people looked up to him as their protector and the person who would ensure that their life became easier and better.

Perhaps his greatest achievement was to found a party that was above racial strife, but when he was forced to resign power in 1964, hundreds of people had died, been wounded, or lost their property in three years of ever worsening civil strife. He was by this time so far away from reality that his government had ceased to care whether those who voted it into power lived or died. He did not even take the trouble to use the money allocated to him by the British Government in 1964 for the country's development.

It would be a tragic personal story if there were not so many innocent people who had suffered. It would be tragic also if one could forget the years of great unemployment and the filthy slums so many were condemned to live and die in. If there is a tragedy, it is in a man who started with an ideal and lost it somewhere about 1956.

The *Guiana Graphic* in August reported that at Aurora on the Essiquibo coast, Dr Jagan told a public meeting, 'I have lived to see many a king fall and I will live to see Burnham and this government fall.'

To this a section of the crowd shouted, 'You have lived to see yourself fall.'

One is left wondering, if Guyana is to move forward, must it really go back through all those Jagan years again?

SELECT BIBLIOGRAPHY

(Official reports, and publications issued in the name of political parties are listed separately.)

Ayearst, Morley. *The British West Indies: The Search for Self-Government.* London, Allen & Unwin, 1960.

Bhagwan, Moses. *Hitler's Force in Guiana.* New Guiana Co. Ltd., Georgetown, 1962.

——*Riot Commission Report Examined.* New Guiana Co. Ltd., Georgetown, 1962.

Bolingbroke, Henry. *A Voyage to the Demerary* (1779-1806). Stevenson & Matchett, Norwich, U.K. (Guiana Edition, no. 1, Georgetown.)

Bradley, C. Paul. 'The Party System in British Guiana and the General Election of 1961', *Caribbean Studies,* October 1961.

Burnham, Forbes L. *The First Hundred Days of Consultative Democracy under the People's National Congress—United Force Government.* British Guiana Lithographic Co. Ltd. 1965.

Cameron, N. E. *The Evolution of the Negro.* Georgetown, Argosy Co. Ltd., 1934.

Campbell, Sir Jock. 'The Development and Organisation of Bookers', paper delivered at the London School of Economics, November 1959.

Carter, Martin. *Poems of Resistance from British Guiana.* London, Lawrence & Wishart, 1954.

Chalmers, Robert (Baron). *A History of Currency in the British Colonies.* London, H.M.S.O., 1893.

Chamberlain. *Smith of Demerara.* London 1924.

Chase, Ashton. *133 Days Towards Freedom in Guiana.* Georgetown, B's Printers, (probably late 1953).

Clements, Sir Cecil. *A Constitutional History of British Guiana,* Macmillan, 1937.

——*The Chinese in British Guiana.* Georgetown, Argosy Co., 1915.

Collins, B. A. N. 'The Civil Service of British Guiana in the General Strike of 1963'. *Caribbean Quarterly,* Vol. 10, no. 2. 1964.

Select Bibliography

Des Voeux, Sir William. *Experiences of a Demarara Magistrate, 1863–1869* (including letter of 1870). (Guiana edition, no. 11, Georgetown, 1948).

Edun, Ayube M. *London's Heart-Probe and Britain's Destiny.* London, Arthur Stockwell, n.d.

Farley, R. 'The Rise of the Peasantry in British Guiana', *Social & Economic Studies*, 11/4, 1954.

Fried, Martin H. 'The Chinese in British Guiana', *Social & Economic Studies*, V. (1956).

Gravesande, Laurens Storm van 's. *The Rise of British Guiana*, London, Hakluyt Society, 2 vols., 1911.

Halperin, Ernst. *Racism and Communism in British Guiana*, Massachusetts Institute of Technology, Cambridge, Mass., 1964.

Harris, Wilson. *Palace of the Peacock.* London, Faber & Faber, 1960.

——*The Far Journey of Oudin.* London, Faber & Faber, 1961.

——And other works.

Hartsinck, J. J. 'The Story of the Slave Rebellion in Berbice – 1762', Amsterdam – 1770. Translated by Walter E. Roth. *Journal of the British Guiana Museum and Zoo*, September, 1960.

Hinden, Rita (ed.). *Local Government and the Colonies – A Report to the Fabian Colonial Bureau.* London, 1950.

Hubbard, H. J. M. *The Workers' Study Circle Committee Members Manual.* Georgetown, n.d.

Jagan, C. *Fight for Freedom: Waddington Constitution Exposed.* Georgetown, "National Printers" for Cheddi Jagan. (c. 1953).

——*Bitter Sugar.* Georgetown, n.d. (?1954).

——*Forbidden Freedom.* London, Lawrence & Wishart, 1954.

——*"Secret" Address to P.P.P. Party Congress on December 22, 1956.* (duplicated only).

——*My Credo.* Georgetown, New Guiana Co. Ltd. (?) 1963.

——*British Guiana's Future, Peaceful or Violent?* Georgetown, New Guiana Co. Ltd., 1964.

Jagan, J. 'Civil Liberties in British Guiana', *W.F.T.U. Bulletin*, March 1st – 15th 1953.

——*Election Facts.* Georgetown, Magnet Printery, n.d. (probably 1953.)

——'Towards a Political Civil Service'. Georgetown, *Thunder*, Vol. 14, no. 6, 1963.

Jayawardena, Chandra. *Conflict and Solidarity in a Guianese Plantation.* University of London, 1963.

King, Sidney. *Next Witness – An Appeal to World Opinion.* Labour Advocate Job Printing Dept., Georgetown, July 1962.
Kirke, Henry. *Twenty-five Years in British Guiana.* London, 1898. (Guiana Edition no. 12, Georgetown, 1948).
London Missionary Society (The). *Report of the Proceedings against the late Rev. J. Smith of Demerara.* London, 1824.
Mahraj, Deoroop. Election Manifesto for 1953.
Naipal, V. S. *The Middle Passage.* London, Andre Deutsch, 1962.
——*A House for Mr. Biswas.* London, Andre Deutsch, 1961.
——And other works.
Nath, Dwarka. *A History of the Indians in British Guiana.* London, Nelson, 1950.
Newman, Peter. *British Guiana.* London, Oxford University Press, 1964.
——'Racial Tension in British Guiana', *Race,* May 1962.
——'The Economic Future of British Guiana', *Social & Economic Studies,* Vol. 9, no. 3, September, 1960.
O'Loughlin, C. 'The Economy of British Guiana 1952–56: A National Accounts Study', *Social & Economic Studies* VIII/1, 1959.
——'The Rice Sector in the Economy of British Guiana', *Social & Economic Studies,* VII, 1958.
Raleigh, Sir Walter. *The Discovery of the Large and Beautiful Empire of Guiana,* Reprinted from edition of 1596, edited by Sir R. H. Schomburgh. London, Hakluyt Society, 1848.
Ramkarran. *Towards an Understanding of the Race Problem.* Published for the Education & Research Committee of the P.P.P. by New Guiana Co. Ltd., Georgetown, March 1963.
Reno, Philip. *The Ordeal of British Guiana.* New York, Monthly Review Press, 1964.
Rodway, J. *Guiana; British, Dutch and French.* London, Unwin, 1912.
——*History of British Guiana from 1668.* Georgetown, 1891–94.
——*The Story of Georgetown.* Georgetown, Argosy Co., 1920.
Roth, Vincent. *Where Is It? A Gazetteer of British Guiana.* Daily Chronicle.
Ruhomon, Peter. *A Centenary History of the East Indians in British Guiana, 1838–1938.* (Guiana Edition, no. 10).
Schomburgh, Robert. *A Description of British Guiana, 1840–44.* London, Simpkin, Marshall, 1840. (Guiana Edition, no. 17, Georgetown, 1922.)

Official Reports

Smith, Raymond T. *British Guiana*. London, Oxford University Press, 1962.
——*The Negro Family in British Guiana*. London, Routledge & Kegan Paul, 1956.
——and C. Jayawardena. 'Marriage and the Family Amongst East Indians in British Guiana', *Social & Economic Studies* viii/4 (1959).
——and C. Jayawardena. 'Hindu Marriage Customs in British Guiana', *Social & Economic Studies* vii/2, 1958.
St. Clair, Thomas Stanton. *A Soldier's Sojourn in British Guiana, 1806–1808*. (Guiana Edition, no. 9. Georgetown, 1947).
Swan, Michael. *British Guiana; The Land of Six Peoples*. London, H.M.S.O., 1957.
——*The Marches of El Dorado*. London, Jonathan Cape, 1958.
Thorne, A. P. 'Some Reflections on British Guiana', *Social & Economic Studies*, Vol. 12, no. 2.
Vatak, Ved Prakash. *British Guiana*, Monthly Review Pamphlet Series – no. 21, 1963.
Wallbridge, Rev. Edwin A. *Demarara Martyr: Memoirs of the Rev. John Smith, 1848*. (Guiana Edition no. 6: 1943).
Waterton, Charles. *Wanderings in South America*. London, Macmillan, 1878.
Webber, A. R. F. *Centenary History and Handbook of British Guiana*. Georgetown, Argosy Co. Ltd. 1931.
Williams, Eric. *The Negro in the Caribbean*. Manchester, Panaf Service, 1944.
Young, Allan. *Approaches to Local Self-Government in British Guiana*. London, Longmans, 1958.

OFFICIAL REPORTS

Report on British Guiana. Annual publication for the Colonial Office, London.
British Guiana Commission, *Report*, Cmd, 2841, 1927.
British Guiana Constitution Commission, *Report*, H.M.S.O. 2985, 1927.
Memorandum prepared by the Elected Members of the Combined Court of British Guiana to the report of the British Guiana Commission (Cmd. 2841) H.M.S.O. 3047, 1928.
Financial Situation in British Guiana, *Report*, Cmd. 3938, 1931.
Memorandum on the Financial Position of British Guiana 1920–46. by O. A. Spencer, British Guiana Government publication.

Enmore Commission, *Report*, Legislative Council No. 10/1948 (foolscap duplicated), 1948.
Commission of Inquiry into the Sugar Industry of British Guiana, *Report*, Col. No. 249, 1949.
British Guiana Constitutional Commission, 1950–51, *Report*, Col. 280, 1951.
Conference on West Indian Federation, *Report*, Cmd. 8837, 1953.
British Guiana; Suspension of the Constitution, *Report*, Cmd. 8980, 1953. ...
The Plan for British Caribbean Federation Cmd. 8895, 1953.
British Guiana Constitutional Commission, *Report*, Cmd. 9274, 1954.
Local Government in British Guiana, *Report*, by A. H. Marshall, Georgetown, Argosy, 1955.
Report of the Government of British Guiana on Employment, Unemployment and Underemployment in the Colony in 1956, by E. McGale, I.L.O. Geneva, 1957.
Commission to review Wages, Salaries & Conditions of Service in the Public Services of British Guiana, 1958–59. (L. H. Gorsuch). British Guiana Government Publication.
British Guiana Development Programme, *Report*, by Kenneth Berrill, British Guiana Sessional Paper 2/1960.
British Guiana Constitutional Conference, *Report*, Cmd. 998, 1960.
British Guiana Constitutional Instruments, 1961, for British Guiana Government 1961.
Commission of Inquiry into Disturbances in British Guiana in February, 1962, *Report*, Col. 354, 1962.
British Guiana Independence Conference, *Report*, Cmd. 1870, 1962.
British Guiana Conference 1963, *Report*, Cmd. 2203, 1963.
Financial Position, *Report*, by K. C. Jacobs. Col. 358, 1964.

PARTY PUBLICATIONS

P.N.C.
——*Legislative Record, 1957–1961*. (duplicated) 1961.
——*Policy on writing a Constitution for an Independent Guiana*, (duplicated) 1962.
——*on the Guillebaud Report* (duplicated) 1962.
P.P.P.
    Constitution, ratified and adopted by the First Congress, Georgetown, Arcade Printery, 1951, (also reprinted and amended, 1962).

Party Publications

1953 Election Manifesto, Georgetown, Charles Packword, 1953.
On Guard, pamphlet, Georgetown Arcade Printery, 1953.
No Constitution, No Christmas, pamphlet, Arcade Printery, 1953.
The Great Betrayal, Georgetown, Arcade Printery, 1st ed. September 1955, 2nd ed. February 1956.
1957 Election Manifesto, Georgetown, 1957.
Independence Now! Georgetown, Arcade Printery, 1960.
1961 Election Manifesto, Georgetown, New Guiana Company, 1961.
P.P.P.s fight for Free Elections, Georgetown, New Guiana Company, 1961.
History of the P.P.P. Georgetown, New Guiana Co. Ltd. 1963.

U.F.

British Guiana: 10 p.p. (duplicated), giving background account of Guiana and the creation of the U.F., n.d., probably early 1962.
Economic Dynamism . . . and You, U.F. 1961 election manifesto, La Penitence, 1961.

INDEX

Abraham, Arthur, 175
Africa, 177
Alfred, David, 91 96
American Indians; *see* Amerindians
Amerindians, 19, 27, 29; first contact with the West, 33–4; political leanings, 148
Andersen, Peter, 9
Annibourne, Neville, 142
Asafu-Adjaye, Sir Edward, 159

Bartica, 33
Bayliss, Sylvia, 9
Beharry, Edward, 143–5
Benn, Brindley 81, 166, 169, 173–81
Bhagwan, Moses, 9, 166, 175–81
Black Fridays, 160, 167, 168
'Blackman', 56–9
Blackman, Carl, 9, 158
Bobb, Lewis, 9
Booker's (Booker Brothers, McConnell & Company, Ltd), 64, 65, 128
Bowman, Fred, 131
British, 9; settlers & planters, 34, 35, 40; Abolition of Slavery, 44–46; Indentured labourers, 49; position in society, 62; Ayube Edun's views, 75–8; Labour Party, 81, 125, 147, 186; government views on Enmore, 97; government views on Venn Commission, 100; White Paper, 112; troops despatched, 121, 125; Conservative government, 125; Government, 128, 132–5, 186, 187; Jagan's attitude, 141, 144, 145; troops, 161, 168; Moses Bhagwan's visit, 179; Jagan's tactics against, 183
Buccra, 21, 58
Budget, 156–60
Burnham, Jessie, 109
Burnham, L. F. S., 9, 68, 98, 147, 169; party leadership, 25; in Parliament, 56; political affiliations, 82; effect of Enmore, 94; PPP leadership, 104, 106; leadership dispute & government posts, 105–10; 1953 Government, 111–21; PPP split, 126–32; views on party ideology, 131, 132; Jagans on, 135–8; forms PNC, 141; starts NYPM, 143; refuses to merge with PPP, 146; and UF & PPP, 149–54; political reappraisal, 155–6; 1961 riots, 158, 160; national front proposal, 166; unemployment demonstration, 167; London 1963, 172; Ghanaian Mission, 173 174; asked to form a government, 176; as Prime Minister, 183–7

Campbell, Sir Jock, 9, 64, 128
Campbell, Stephen, 140
Caribbean Conference, 174
Carter, John, 9, 134, 138, 142
Carter, Keith, 110
Carter, Martin, 7, 9, 110, 131
Castro, Fidel, 173
Chandisingh, Ranji, 10, 166, 167
Chase, Ashton, 10, 80, 107–9, 112, 113, 121, 126, 166, 178, 179
Chicago, 69
China, 61, 70, 179
Chinese, 19, 29; indentured labourer, 50; in relation to other peoples, 59–65
Civil Disobedience, 77, 128
Civil Service, 60, 68, 142, 146, 148, 157, 159, 170, 184
Civil Service Association (CSA), 143, 156, 159, 168
Collins, Bertram, 10
Columbus, Christopher, 33
Commission: Constitutional (1954), 82; Enmore, 91, 96, 97; Venn, 35, 51, 97, 100; Robertson, 100, 102, 126–9; Waddington, 100, 101; 172; Renison Constitutional, 145; Inquiry into Disturbances (1962), 154; Gorsuch, 156; Wynn Parry, 159, 160
Communications: transport, 31
Communism: and the voter, 25
Communist Party: USA, 70; GB

Index

West Indies Committee, 74; GB and PAC, 82; GB, 97; Soviet Union, 142; China, 179
Constitution: 1953, suspension of, 24, 52, 78-9; 1947, 100; Waddington, 101, 111, 134; Renison's proposals (1956) 133, 134; Renison in practice, 141; Conference (1960), 146; 1962, 165; Independence Conference (1965 London), 181
Coolie, 56-9
Copenhagen, 115
Creole gangs, 51
Critchlow, H. M., 75
Croker, Jake, 10
Crown Lands, sale forbidden, 54
Cuba, 173, 179

d'Aguiar, Peter, 9, 147, 150, 152, 153, 159, 160, 170, 174; 1961 riots, 154, 156-8, 161, 162; background & politics, 147, 148
Des Voeux, Sir G. William, 52, 53
Downer, Victor, 175
Doyle, Conan, 28
Drayton, Evan, 10
'drivers', 51
Dutch, 61, 117; first settlers, 33-4; settlers, 43
Dutt, Palme, 74

Edun, Ayube, 75, 85
El Dorado, 27, 30
El Dorado Youth Alliance (PNC), 143
Elections: average electoral percentages, 20; 1964, 25; 1947, 83; 1957, 140, 141; 1953, 140; 1961, 151, 152; 1964, 175
Enmore, 144; riots, 51, 89-95, 106, 186
Estates, 21, 184; beginnings, 35, 36; ownership of, 38; change to indentured labour, 50; lack of medical care, 53; change in life under indenture system, 50-65
Europeans, 31, 34

Faloon, Mr, 45
Fawcett, Colonel, 27
Federation of Unions of Government Employees 156, 159, 168
Fernandes, 'Honest' John, 84
Freedom March, 174
'Freedom Riders', 168

Gaskin, Winifred, 83, 150
Georgetown, 29, 36, 39, 54, 71, 72, 91, 94, 96, 99, 122-4, 126, 127, 133-5, 140, 149-51, 155, 158, 160-5, 167, 174; physical features, 31; Queen's College, 63, 68; 1947 elections, 84
General Strike: 1963, 79; 1953, 124
German: indentured labourers, 49
Ghana, 173; Mission, 174
Governments: Interim, 135, 140; 1957, 141; 1961, 151 et seq
Great Betrayal, 128, 130
Grey, Sir Ralph, 161
Guiana Agricultural Workers Union, 166, 174, 175, 180
Guiana Industrial Workers Union, 78, 80, 89, 90, 94, 96, 117, 118, 120, 166
Gocking, W. E., 10
Guiana Sugar Workers Union, 166
Guillebaud, Mr, (Commission), 156
Guyana: historical influences, 19 et seq.; racial influences, 22 et seq.; physical features, 27, et seq.; meaning of name, 28; industries, 30; size & population, 19, 30; demographic problems, 30-32; first settlers, 33 et seq.; land reclamation, 34-5; diseases, 43
Guyana Independence Movement, 145

Hands-Jakeway, 156
Harlow, V., 101
Harris, Wilson, 7
Hart, R. B. O., 98, 128, 129
Hart, Richard, 10
Hill, Frank, 132
Hinden, Rita, 101
Hogben, Lancelot, 10
Hong Kong, 61
House of Assembly, see Parliament
Hubbard, Jocelyn, 10, 74, 75, 78, 80, 84, 94, 95, 173
Hucksters, 41, 59, 81; loss of trade, 60
Hungary, 133, 179

Indentured Labourers, 21, 27, 49-55; English, German, Portuguese & West Indians, 49; general system & pay, 50
Independent Labour: 1947 election, 83
India, 48, 57, 126; government agrees to indenture system, 50
Indians, 19, 24, 25; indentures, 50, 55; money saved after indenture, 54; views on the other peoples, 56-60; relationship with Negro, 81; 1947 elections, 84; effect of

195

Enmore, 94; and MPCA, 102; PPP views on landlords, 136 and estate workers, 137; Federation, 139; political leanings, 147, 154; racial animosity, 174, 175; support for PPP, 177
Ishmael, Richard, 160, 166

Jackson, Andrew, 10
Jackson, Sir Donald, 126, 145
Jardim, Ann, 10
Jagan, Cheddi: background, 19–21; ideology, 21; 1953 election victory, 24; 1953–1964 leadership, 24; instigates social change, 58, 64. 65; youth & education, 66–73; Marxist-Leninist philosophy, 71; enters politics, 74–85; and Trade Unions, 75, 78–80; and Communist Party (GB), 82; 1947 elections, 83; and Legislative Council, 86, 87; Enmore, 89–95; and Enmore Commission, 96; visit to Eastern Europe (1951), 100; *Forbidden Freedom*, 105–22; dispute over party leadership & government posts, 105–10; 1953 government, 111–21; and Communist literature, 115, 116; Suspension of Constitution (1963), 121–5; 'Secret' Speech (1956), 125, 134–9, 141; to London & India, 125, 126; PPP split, 126–32; *Daily Gleaner* interview, 140; Minister for Trade, 141; to London with Governor, 143; to Canada, 144; to Britain for aid, 145; UF & PNC, 149–54; US visit, 152–3; 1961 riots, 158–61; national front proposal, 165, 166; parliamentary suspension, 170; letter to Sandys, 171; PPP split, 177–83; to London, Eastern Europe & Cuba, 179–80; Party Congress, 180, 181; boycott of Independence Conference, 181, 182; his career, 185–7
Jagan, Janet: marriage & arrival in Guyana, 69–73; enters politics, 74–85; and trade unions, 75, 78–80; 1947 elections, 83; loss of American nationality, 85; Enmore, 89–95; and Enmore Commission, 96; General Secretary, 98; PPP victory speech, 105; dispute over party leadership & government posts, 105–10; Deputy Speaker, 109; 1953 government, 111–21; to Copenhagen & Roumania, 115; Suspension of Constitution (1953), 121–5; PPP split, 126, 132,; Ministry for Labour, 141–2; Bhagwan's comments, 181
Jagan, Mrs (mother of Dr Jagan), 67, 68
Jamaica, 122
Jeffrey, Lionel, 131

Kaldor, Dr Nicholas, 156
Kelshall, Jack, 10, 153, 159
Kendall, W. O., 114, 140, 143, 169
Khosla, Justice Gopal Das, 159
King, Sidney, 107, 108, 110, 112, 113, 118
Kykoveral, 33

La Bonne Intention, 90
Labour Party (BG), 81, 102; 1947 elections, 84, 85; 1947 programme, 86, 87, 88
Labour Relations Bill (1953), 78, 119, 121, 123; (1963), 167, 170; future, 171
Labour Union (B.G.), 75
Lachhmansingh, Dr, 78, 84, 91, 96, 97, 105–7, 110, 117, 118, 129, 135
Lall, Harry, 175
Law; planters as Magistrates, 52
Legislative Assembly and Legislative Council: see Parliament
L'Enterprise, 46
Le Resouvenir, 39, 42
Lethem, Sir Gordon, 62, 80
Lewis, Sir Arthur, 185
London Missionary Society, 39
Luckhoo, Lionel, 10, 135, 175
Luyt, Sir Richard, 176

MacDonald, Ian, 10
McLeod, Superintendent, 162
Manoa, 27
Manpower Citizens Association, 75, 78–80, 89–91, 102, 115, 118, 159, 166; 1947 elections, 83, 84
Mao Tse Tung, 125, 139, 141
Moral Rearmament (MRA), 148
Morris, William, 98
Nasser, President, 144
National Democratic Party; elections (1953), 103
National Labour Front, 135, 140, 145, 148
National Young People's Movement (PNC), 143
Negro, 19, 24, 25, 29, 31; as slaves, 34–43; emancipation & subsequent experiences, 44–9, 54; free villages, 46, 47; indentured

Index

labourers, 50; influence of the past, 56; views on other peoples, 56–65; relationship with Indian, 81; and PPP, 82; 1947 elections, 84; effect of Enmore, 94; Labour Party, 102; Negro vote, 110, 129, 179; West Indian Negro, 132; Federation, 139; Civil Service, 142; with relation to the UF, 149; image, 151; racial animosity, 174; 'Negro Menace', 176
Nehru, J., Prime Minister, 126, 144
New Amsterdam, 54
New China News Agency, 179
New Nation (PNC), 141
New York, 69
Nicholson, Dr J. A., 84
Nkrumah, K., President, 144
Non Pareil, 90–92

Parliament, 56, 80, 84, 86–9, 101, 102, 104, 113, 115–17, 119, 123, 145, 146; Recall System, 84
Pegasse, 35
'Peoples' Council of Ministers', 116
'Peoples Government', 121
People's National Congress (PNC), 83, 143, 146, 148, 149, 155, 160, 161, 165, 166, 169, 171, 172, 174, 176; foundation of, 141; UDP merger, 145; UF & PPP, 148–54; 1961 elections, 151–2; 1964 elections, 175
People's National Party, 103
Peoples Progressive Party, 26, 56, 100, 102, 155, 156; agitation, 24, 25; 1953 government, 52; social importance, 58; 1953 & 1957 electoral victories, 62; international view, 71; appears as a National Liberation party, 81; organization, 98–100; and Waddington Commission, 101; Elections 1953, 103, 104; 1953 electoral victory, 105; Party Congress (1953), 106; leadership dispute & government posts, 105–9; 1953 government, 106; National Front Movement, 108, 110; Peoples Government, 114; Women's Political & Economic Organization (W.P. & E. O.), 83; Women's Progressive Organization (WPO), 115, 180; Suspension of Constitution (1953), 126; Civil Disobedience Campaign, 128; split, 126–32; Annual Congress, 1956, 134–9; Manifesto 1957, 139; Elections 1957, 140; Youth Rally, 142; 1961 elections, 151–2; coalition with PNC talks, 165; after 1961 riots, 164, 165; 1964 elections, 175; reaction to elections, 177–83; Congress (1965), 180, 181
Pilgrim Fathers, 33
Pilgrim, Frank, 10
Plantations see Estates
Political Affairs Committee, 71, 84, 89, 94, 96, 97, 186; objectives, 80; Georgetown support, 81; and Scientific Socialism & electioneering, 83; political influence 85; Enmore, 94
Pollock, Venetia, 10
Pork-knocker, 29–30, 61
Portuguese, 19, 24, 29; indentured labourers, 49–50; in relation to other peoples, 59–65; indentures & afterwards, 59; 1947 elections, 84
Progressive Youth League, 166
Progressive Youth Movement (PYM), 109
Progressive Youth Organization (PYO), 143, 178, 180, 181; Congress, (1963), 173, 177
Proportional Representation, 25, 146, 177, 182, 183

Quaison-Sackey, 173

Raleigh, Sir Walter, 27
Ramkarran, 10, 113, 114, 181
Ramphal, 'Sonny', 185
Ramsahoye, Dr Fenton, 10
Rangela, Amos, 78
'ranges', 21, 52
Rational - Practical - Ideal State (R.P.I.), 77–8
Recall System, 84
Renison, Sir Patrick, 133, 141, 142
Rice, 54, 58
Rice Farmers' Security and Tenure Bill, 116
Rice Marketing Board (R.M.B.), 54, 167, 170
Riots, 19; 1961, 157; 1963, 167 et seq.
Robertson, George, 131
Robertson, Sir James, 126
Rosenberg, Janet, 70
Rosenbergs, 70
Roumania, 115
Russia; see Soviet Union

Saffee, Mohammed, 170, 180
Sandys, Duncan, 171–3, 182
Savage, Sir Alfred, 113

Sawmill & Forest Workers' Union, 117
Schuler, Leon, 84
Scientific Socialism, 81
Searwar, Lloyd, 10
Sharples, Dr Leon, 106
Singh Adjoha, 114
Singh, Jai Naraine, 109, 110, 129, 145
Singh, Dr J. B., O.B.E., 81
Singh, Ricky, 10
Slavery, abolition of, 21; general account, 34–43; abolition of trading and later owning, 44; attempt at apprenticeship, 46; compensation, 46; emancipation, 49
Slaves, 27, 34; personal economy, 59
Smith, Ferdinand, 138
Smith, John, 39–42
Smith, Raymond, 81
South Africa, 132
Soviet Union, 70, 135, 145; Edun's views, 77; Radio Moscow, 152
Stalin, Joseph, 125, 131, 137
Stabroek, 36
State of Emergency, 175
Strachan, Billy, 138
Strikes, 1953, 118, 119, 124
Sugar Producers' Association (SPA), 90, 91, 117, 118, 176
Surinam, 34

Tito, President, 131
Thomas, Clive, 10
Thompson, Adrian, 10
Thompson, Laurence, 10
Thunder, 71, 97, 99, 113

Trades Union Congress (B.G.-T.U.C), 121, 143, 146, 159, 160, 163, 167, 168

Undesirable Publications Bill (Prohibition of Importation), 115, 116
United Democratic Party (U.D.P.), 134, 135, 137, 140, 143, 145, 148
United Farmers & Workers Party, 103
United Force (U.F.), 26, 159, 148, 149, 155, 156, 159, 165, 171, 175, 176, 185; composition, 26; formation and the PPP, 148, 154; 1961 elections, 151–2; 1964 elections, 175
United Guiana Party, elections 1953, 103
United Nations (U.N.), 144, 173

Van Sertima, 109
Venn, J. A., 97
Village shops, 60

West Africa, social effects of slavery, 37
West Indian Federation, 139
Westmass, Rory, 105, 110, 131
Wong, Clinton, 107, 108, 109, 111, 130
Woodcock, George, 126
Workers' Study Circles, 75
World Peace Council (Preparatory Committee) (W.P.C.), 179
World Federation of Democratic Youth, 179

Young, Allan, 10, 47
Young Communist League, 70

For Product Safety Concerns and Information please contact our EU
representative GPSR@taylorandfrancis.com
Taylor & Francis Verlag GmbH, Kaufingerstraße 24, 80331 München, Germany

www.ingramcontent.com/pod-product-compliance
Lightning Source LLC
Chambersburg PA
CBHW061447300426
44114CB00014B/1867